Within 20 years the right to drive may be restricted by the use of a special driving permit ... Suddenly the world is awakening to the fact that the modern 20th Century miracles in manufacturing may become mausoleums for the future.

* * *

Civilization as we know it is fading into the horizon. We have squandered our resources and polluted our environment to a point of no return.

* * *

Soon Americans will be eating less nutritional-value food and more "analog" foods ... foods that are similar in looks but not in origin. American diets will soon be taking a drastic change and not for the better.

* * *

It took all of recorded history for the world to produce its first billion inhabitants around 1850. Then 80 years were needed to pass the 2 billion mark in 1930. Another 31 years to reach 3 billion in 1961. But only 15 years were required to add the 4th billion in 1976!

* * *

In the 1976 Olympics in Montreal security controls cost well over $100 million! This made Montreal Olympics the most expensive security operation in history. Security averaged $8000 per athlete!

* * *

Violence and vandalism in the nation's public schools are approaching epidemic proportions. In Chicago a budget of $10 million must be allocated just to stablize disorder in schools!

* * *

Computerized markings on food products will soon generate a new way of buying without cash. Whoever can control the computer can control human life.

* * *

There is a definite trend in evangelization to imitate the world; in programming, in music and in presentation ... Some believe there is a trend towards conglomerates for Christ. Big is considered good while small is considered bad.

* * *

What action prompted the Cambridge, Massachusetts City Council to urge Harvard University to stop construction on a new one-half million dollar science laboratory? Would such research affect mankind?

* * *

Under contract with the National Science Foundation, a group of scientists sit at the world's largest radio telescope in Puerto Rico, reading messages from stars and broadcasting advertisements for the human race.

* * *

The Common Market nations are growing at a more rapid rate than their competitors. And their power is increasing. Is this an indication of the prophetic fulfillment of Daniel's 10 nation league?

* * *

Half of the world's scientists are now employed on improving existing weapons and developing new ones (laser death ray, nerve gas, etc.).

COUNTDOWN
9876543210
TO RAPTURE
by Salem Kirban

Second Printing . . . Completely updated . . . . . September, 1980

Published by SALEM KIRBAN, Inc., Kent Road, Huntingdon Valley, Penna. 19006. Copyright© 1977, 1980 by Salem Kirban. Printed in the United States of America. All rights reserved, including the right to reproduce this book or portions thereof in any form.

Library of Congress Catalog Card No. 77-79681
ISBN 0-912582-26-X

DEDICATION

Wes takes Jessica and Joshua for a walk in the woods.

Doreen

Duane

To our daughter DOREEN, who was willing to leave 20th Century conveniences behind to pioneer. She and her husband Wes Frick moved to a one-room rustic cabin he helped build on a mountain in Valley, Washington in 1976. Although it had no running water nor a kitchen sink they discovered the joys of getting back to nature and living close to God.

To our son DUANE, who graduated from high school in 1977 and enters into a world of change ... a world that may witness the Rapture in his lifetime.

To L. E. MAXWELL and T. S. RENDALL and PRAIRIE BIBLE INSTITUTE. In an era when many Christian churches and schools are trying to emulate the world, Prairie Bible Institute stands out as one of the few remaining testimonies that dares to stand for old fashioned principles.

Prairie Bible Institute uses the Bible as its textbook. Although some may in error believe their methods archaic, they prepare lives steeled for service through discipline. Training disciplined soldiers for Christ since 1922, this interdenominational school is now one of the largest in North America with over 800 students.

President Maxwell delivers diploma to 1977 graduate. Prairie Bible Institute is at Three Hills, Alberta, Canada.

Diane

Dawn

Over 1800 young people from its 5000 alumni have gone from Prairie Bible Institute to foreign mission fields. Their teachers and staff become their examples of unselfish service and sacrifice. For each employee (from President on down) receives the <u>same</u> very modest salary, regardless of position.
L. E. Maxwell has been its President since its founding in 1925.
T. S. Rendall is Vice-President.

Prairie Bible Institute has grown because of its unique method of Bible study, its Cross-centered curriculum and its spirit of Missions.

Would that more Christian institutions dare to follow Prairie's lead in getting back to the message of Calvary! Prairie is doing its part to hasten the Rapture through training Christian soldiers for the battlefield of world missions.

To our daughter DIANE, who was willing to leave the comforts of home to attend Prairie Bible Institute in Alberta, Canada to train as a disciplined soldier for Christ.

To our daughter DAWN, who, although only 16, has already caught the burden for lost souls and spent the summer of 1977 as a Teen Missionary helping missionaries in Venezuela.

ACKNOWLEDGMENTS

To **Doreen Frick,** who carefully proofread the text.

To **Dr. Gary G. Cohen,** President of Graham Bible College at Bristol, Tennessee, who checked the final manuscript, making many helpful suggestions.

To **Walter W. Slotilock,** Chapel Hill Litho, for skillfully making the illustration negatives.

To **Batsch Company, Inc.,** for excellent craftsmanship in setting the type quickly.

To **Koechel Designs,** who designed the front cover and chapter art.

CONTENTS

SPONSORS

COUNTDOWN TO RAPTURE could not have become a reality without the prayerful dedication of the Lord's money entrusted to God's people. The below Sponsors have shared in the distribution of this book and we are extremely grateful. In some instances the names listed are memorial gifts.

"The Lord gave the Word:
great was the company of those that published it."
(Psalm 68:11)

WHY I WROTE THIS BOOK

We are living in an age of change . . . rapid change. Perhaps the very fact that changes are occurring so quickly dulls one's senses to realize actually what is happening to this world!

Most of the changes are not for the better. They are changes that are preparing us for the Last Days, the Rapture and the awesome judgments during the 7-year Tribulation Period.

Whether or not one accepts the Bible as the Word of God, does not alter the fact that the world is facing imponderable problems . . . problems, which in the opinion of this author, are unsolvable by man. We have reached the point of no return. We are on an irreversible course for world disaster.

If one looks honestly at the changes that are occurring, regardless of one's spiritual beliefs, one can see a frightening picture developing for tomorrow's world. It is my hope that this book, COUNTDOWN TO RAPTURE, will help crystallize these changes by focusing on them in a concentrated fashion.

I am an investigative reporter. My background includes covering the Vietnam War as a war correspondent and also the 6-Day War in Israel. Each week I personally research through some 300 publications (from all areas of the globe) and clip those articles which have prophetic significance and give some indication, no matter how subtle, of a changing world.

COUNTDOWN TO RAPTURE is the synthesis of this research. For those not familiar with the term "Rapture," it is a term used by those who accept the Bible as the literal Word of God.

RAPTURE refers to the time, prior to the start of the 7 year Tribulation Period, when believing Christians (both dead and alive) will "in the twinkling of an eye" rise up to meet Christ in the air. See 1 Thessalonians 4:14-17 in the New Testament portion of the Bible.

After this Rapture comes a holocaust of judgments never before witnessed by man. **COUNTDOWN TO RAPTURE,** in part, serves to inform you that this world is changing and that the stage is already being set for this final world catastrophe which will culminate in the Battle of Armageddon . . . a battle where 200 million will die!

In the Old Testament in Daniel 9:25 we learn that a world leader known as Antichrist will be successful in making vast world changes. He will be able to change laws and to change customs. Among his changes will be changes from individual freedom to a controlled life. One will no longer be able to go to a supermarket and make purchases freely. This will be a change . . . for the worse. To purchase goods or to sell, it will be necessary for any individual first to swear his loyalty to Antichrist and bear his mark of allegiance either on his right hand or forehead.

Changes in our spiritual standards are already paving the way for Antichrist. Such changes will make it also possible for a world religious leader to come on the scene during the Tribulation Period and direct further allegiance to his leader, Antichrist. That man will be known as the False Prophet.

In the motion picture, Three Comrades, produced in the late 1930's, Margaret Sullivan turned to Robert Taylor and said:

> *I was just thinking something foolish . . . thinking how nice it would be if we could pick a time to be born.*

As the stress and strain of today's living takes its toll, many will wish they had an option to pick a time to be born. Perhaps many will long for the rather simple, uncomplicated days of the post-World War 2 era of the 1940's and 1950's. But those days are gone forever!

Each day sees more change take place. Sure we can land Viking 1 on Mars via remote control and send back color photographs. But it still is a project to mail a letter and expect it to be delivered in a reasonable length of time . . . even across one's own city! The paradox of 20th century advancements is that really, the more we progress . . . the more we regress!

It was Heraclitus that said:

> There is nothing permanent but change.

Faith Baldwin believed that: "Time is a dressmaker specializing in alterations."

You may remember Tennyson's *Passing of Arthur* in which he wrote: "The old order changeth, yielding place to the new."

COUNTDOWN TO RAPTURE concerns itself with 11 major areas of changes that we believe are critical and are a prelude to the Tribulation Period.

> Changes in WORLD ENVIRONMENT
> Changes in WORLD RESOURCES
> Changes in VALUES
> Changes in THE QUALITY OF LIFE
> Changes in HEALTH CARE
> Changes in THE ECONOMY
> Changes in SPIRITUAL STANDARDS
> Changes in SCIENCE CAPABILITIES
> Changes in MINOR WORLD POWERS
> Changes in MAJOR WORLD POWERS
> Changes in MIDDLE EAST BALANCE OF POWER

Job, in the midst of his suffering, was surrounded by three counselors who offered him no compassion. They were like the proverbial "friend" who visits you in the hospital and tells you she remembers someone with the same disease who died. Eliphaz reproves Job, accusing him of sin:

> Is not thy wickedness great?
> and thy iniquities infinite? (Job 22:5)

Job had tremendous wealth for those days: 7000 sheep, 3000 camels, 500 yoke of oxen and 500 donkeys. Yet he lost them all. Job was an example of patience and devotion to God. He lost his wealth, he lost his friends. He even lost the support of his wife when she told him:

Curse God, and die.
(Job 2:9)

Yet despite the changes in his life pattern ... changes that would overwhelm most of us, his unchanging faith in God remained steadfast when he stated:

Though He slay me, yet will I trust in Him ...
(Job 13:15)

And his assurance during his troubled times is summed up in Job 19:25, 26:

For I know that my Redeemer liveth,
and that He shall stand at the latter day upon the earth.
Even after my skin is destroyed,
Yet from my flesh I shall see God!

In this world of rapid change towards self-destruction, it is my hope that you will come to trust the God that changes not as the One who took your sin upon Himself on the cross. By accepting Christ as your personal Saviour and Lord, you can change your destination from an eternity in hell to an eternity in Heaven!

Change and decay in all around I see,
O Thou, who changest not, abide with me!
Salem Kirban

Huntingdon Valley, Pennsylvania U.S.A.
July, 1977

P.S.   We are now in the 1980's and the problems that I defined in 1977 when I wrote this book are now even greater! We are rapidly headed for a world holocaust and the soon coming Rapture!

14

CHANGES IN WORLD ENVIRONMENT

11:57

❝ We may even have to acknowledge that the individual's right to use his private vehicle is no longer absolute. ❞
William T. Coleman
U.S. Secretary of Transportation
(in a speech to a convention of the
American Automobile Association)

COUNTDOWN 11:57 TO RAPTURE

AIR POLLUTION

Deadly Smog Increasing

It was early August, 1975. The east coast of the United States was suffering from a week of hot, sticky days. A stagnant mass of foul air, settled over an area extending from southern Michigan to New York City . . . and southward to North Carolina.

Over 75 million Americans were caught in the clutch of the worst blanket of pollution recorded by the National Weather Service since November, 1962.

Washington, D.C. was the worst hit as many were left gasping . . . elderly died, their death accelerated by the smog blanket that robbed them of their very breath. The District of Columbia daily spews 2400 tons of pollution from motor vehicles every workday. This alone produces over 95% of the carbon monoxide and 79% of the hydrocarbons in the city's air.

Los Angeles has an annual smog season. It is not unusual for them to suffer through 40-50 smog alerts each year.

The Day They Ban Automobiles

The U.S. Environmental Protection Agency has discussed the possibility of banning cars from large center-city areas. Los Angeles has speed lanes for those who drive on the expressways with 3 or more passengers.

Within 20 years the right to drive may be restricted by the use of a special driving permit.

In Seveso, Italy, where leaking gas from a chemical plant polluted the atmosphere, health department workers collect the bodies of animals killed by the poisonous fumes. The entire town was evacuated. One day such a tragedy may kill thousands of humans.

**Ozone
Can
You
See**

Suddenly the world is awakening to the fact that modern 20th Century miracles in manufacturing may become mausoleums for the future. The popular aerosol spray that uses fluorcarbons is now banned.

Aerosol sprays affect the ozone layer which serves as a protective shield for humans. In nature, ozone is formed by the ultraviolet light in sunshine reacting with the oxygen in the earth's atmosphere. Oxygen exposed to ultraviolet light converts to ozone — a gaseous molecule of three atoms of oxygen.

**Natural
Ozone
A
Protective
Shield**

The natural ozone in the atmosphere protects life on earth by absorbing lethal doses of the sun's ultraviolet radiation. This ozone in maximum concentration is found in a band about 22 miles above the earth.

If you could squeeze all the natural ozone in the air together, this entire quantity would only form a layer just fractions of an inch thick!

Natural ozone in the atmosphere protects life on earth from lethal doses of the sun's ultraviolet radiation by absorbing it.

**Man-Made
Ozone
Destroys
The Shield**

Man-made ozone pollutes the air when it forms faster than nature can get rid of it. It changes our environment soiling the air with irritating and destructive gases. It is the culprit in smog that makes the eyes sting and literally eats away some materials.

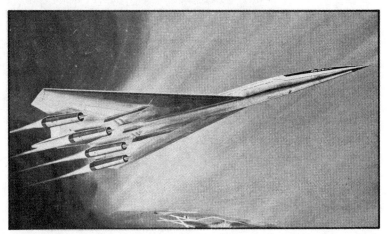

Will these supersonic jets destroy the ozone protective shield around the earth? Will this contribute to the oppressive heat in the Fourth Vial that allows the sun to scorch all mankind (Revelation 16:8-9)?

Twentieth Century progress included the introduction of the aerosol spray. For 30 years the aerosol spray has been an ever-increasing part of everyday life. Many scientists believe we will now suffer the consequences of ozone depletion with an increase in skin cancer and drastic changes in our weather patterns and temperatures.

Supersonic Jets Compound the Problem

With the introduction of the English-French Concorde SST and the Soviet Tupolov-144 SST came heated debates on increased air pollution. No one knows for sure whether these supersonic jets will destroy the ozone protective shield that surrounds the earth. The problem: it would take 10 years of study just to see a trend in ozone destruction and it would take 100 years to correct the damage done!

Skin Cancer To Increase

Scientists estimate that just a 5% ozone depletion could cause over 60,000 more cases of skin cancer in the United States. The year 1990 is the year scientists indicate that such a 5% drop in ozone will have occured.

To further complicate the problem . . . to grow more food to feed an expanding population, we entered into a Green Revolution using multiple thousands of tons of nitrogen fertilizer. A byproduct of this nitrogen application is nitrous oxide, N_2O. Nitrous oxide destroys the ozone protective layer above the earth.

To Eat Or Not To Eat

The dilemma: How are we to increase fertilizer use to improve the quality of life, sustain population growth . . . when the very use of that fertilizer destroys ozone and our ability to sustain life?

Yet to meet food needs over the next 25 years, projections of nitrogen fertilizer use have been suggested as high as ten times present usage! Such facts would seem to indicate that the end times are very, very near and we are on an irreversible course.

21

Even the Acropolis in Athens, Greece has suffered the effects of air pollution. Marble sculptures are being removed.

COUNTDOWN
11:57
TO RAPTURE

AIR POLLUTION

The Sewer in the Sky

A discussion about air pollution doesn't have the same dramatic appeal as the coming battle of Armageddon. Yet the polluting of our atmosphere is like spawning a "sewer in the sky" that silently and slowly will rob us of very life itself.

A Sudden Depletion in Ozone

And while a 5000 megaton war may kill many, many people . . . such an atomic explosion could almost instantaneously reduce the protective ozone shield by some 50 to 75 percent! The illness and death from such destruction would be far more devastating!

Pennsylvania Cows Eat China's Pollution

It was hard for those in the Philadelphia area to believe that an atomic bomb explosion in China in the early fall of 1976 could affect them. Yet the fallout from that explosion drifted across the Pacific and across the United States. Several days of smog and rain hit the eastern seaboard just as this polluted and radiated dust was drifting over the Philadelphia-Washington, D.C. area. The rain carried the radioactive waste down to the earth. The cows ate the radioactive grass and the milk then became contaminated.

The Polluted Acropolis

In Athens, Greece in 1976, the minister of culture allocated $2 million to make duplicates of 2500-year-old statues at the Acropolis. The original marble sculptures will be removed to a museum. **Reason: the monuments have suffered from air pollution alone more in the last 40 years than from all damage received during the past four centuries!**

11:56

66 The President came in here and promised us he would cut the red tape so we could rebuild. But the tape's as thick as ever. Somebody seems to have dropped the scissors. 99
(An individual who lost both his store and his home in a tornado that swept Xenia, Ohio in 1974)

**The Day
Xenia
Collapsed**

One quiet day in Xenia, Ohio in 1974 a funnel cloud hovered over the city and a raging tornado killed 34 persons, leveled more than 1000 homes and left the downtown area a pile of rubble. Government officials from FDAA, HUD, HEW, EPA, SBA, EDA swooped down with myriad forms to fill out. It took two months just to convince the government that $100,000 was needed for a housing study. The people of Xenia soon learned that the wheels of government move slowly — even in disaster.

**The Power
of Water
Unleashed**

In May, 1980, Mt. St. Helens volcano in the state of Washington erupted with a fury that blew about 2000 feet of mountain from its top . . . spewing steam and ash up to 17,000 feet in the air! Over $1 Billion in damage was done!

**Living on
Top of
Disaster**

The San Andreas fault, a fracture in the earth's crust nine miles deep and 650 miles long, keeps Californians in a state of fear. It runs from 100 miles north of San Francisco down to the Mexican border. The earth's surface is made up of land masses called plates. These plates float like rafts. The north-west-bound Pacific plate meets the North American plate at the San Andreas fault. Friction locks the plates together at certain points near San Francisco and Los Angeles, but the rest of the two plates keep moving. It's like pulling on a board that is nailed down at one end. When the pressure builds up . . . the plate lurches . . . the stored energy is released and — EARTHQUAKE!

History's Great Quakes

YEAR	LOCALE	DEATH TOLL
856	Corinth, Greece	45,000
1556	Shensi, China	830,000
1737	Calcutta	300,000
1755	Lisbon	60,000
1883	Dutch Indies	36,000
1902	Martinique	40,000
1906	San Francisco	700
1920	Kansu, China	180,000
1923	Tokyo	143,000
1960	Agadir, Morocco	12,000
1964	Alaska	114*
1970	Peru	67,000
1972	Managua, Nicaragua	10,000
1975	Mukden, China	†

†UNREPORTED, BUT BELIEVED TO BE HIGH

*Although the loss of life was relatively small, this quake was one of the strongest ever measured, with a magnitude of more than 8.4 on the Richter scale.

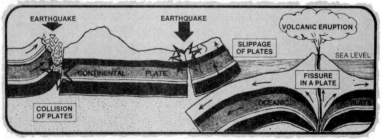

Chart illustrates how an earthquake occurs.

The Bulge Most Everyone Ignores

California Institute of Technology geophysicists have been rather successful in predicting when earthquakes will strike California. In early 1976 they predicted that California would experience an earthquake within 1 year. It did! Geologists are especially concerned about a rise in elevation of up to 10 inches of land along the San Andreas fault over an area of about 4500 square miles. This bulge may be the advance warning of an earthquake of severe magnitude that could leave hundreds or thousands of Californians dead within the next 3-5 years! Yet despite warnings, those living on top of the fault live in casual apathy as though nothing will happen.

Coffinmakers Ran Out of Wood

At 3:04 AM one February day in 1976 an earthquake of 7.5 on the Richter scale hit Managua, Nicaragua. The quake toll left over 22,084 dead and over 75,000 people injured. Guatemalan radio pleaded: "The morgue is full. Please don't bring any more bodies to the morgue." For those who witnessed the scene they said: "It was like the world was ending." Over 200,000 were left homeless. Bodies lay amid the wreckage. At the city's principal cemetery, weeping families had to wait in line to bury dead relatives. Coffinmakers ran out of wood. Food prices skyrocketed. Frantic people were eating rats and anything they could get their hands on.

The Day China Was Moved

In July, 1976, China suffered an earthquake that measured 8.2 on the Richter scale. It is estimated that perhaps 250,000 died.

27

11:57

" ... changes in temperature and rainfall are not ruled out. ...

Climatic Impact Committee
U.S. National Academy of Sciences

We may be moving from the silence of spring to the winter of global death. "

Herb Denenberg
Environmentalist

Are We Reaching The Point of No Return?

Is civilization, as we know it, fading into the horizon? Have we squandered our resources and polluted our environment to a point of no return?

Many experts think so. Some scoff at the doomsday theory but others believe it to be a realistic appraisal of today's situation.

In our food there has been an unrestrained use of dangerous food additives . . . additives that do not show immediate effects but reign their destruction in our children and their children. We have been deep into the age of food additives for 30 years and now the harvest of illness is being reaped.

Continuing pollution by pesticides have infiltrated every part of the globe even to the polar ice cap.

6000 New Chemicals Annually

Worldwide, about 6000 new chemicals are created every year creating uncontrolled pollution by toxic substances.

The Mad Scientists

Scientists all over the world are engaged in gene transplantation. Who knows what a bag of horrors this will unleash!

Enter The Super-Pest!

Various pesticides have released a strain of "super-pests" that have caused crop set backs in Peru, Mexico, Central America and Egypt. In 1976 the Southern pine beetle infested 54 million of the 85 million acres of Southern pine forest in the U.S., killing over 300,000 acres!

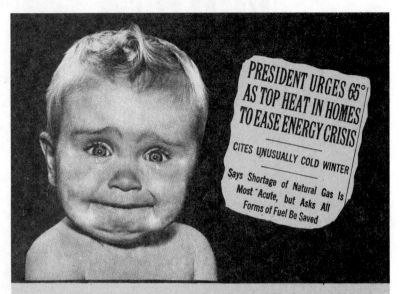

Above ad illustrates reality of fuel crisis. By 1983 large cars will not be manufactured, nor will V-8 engines. General Motors predicts cars will be the size and weight of a Chevrolet Nova.

**And
Not a Drop
To Drink**

It's hard to believe that a nation that receives 700 billion gallons of water from the environment every day could be facing a shortage of consumable water. But it is true! Each day, municipal sewers dump 40 billion gallons into the nation's water resources. Industry discharges 125 billion gallons of waste into the same water each day.

**The
Ocean
Sewer**

We treat our ocean as if it were not part of our planet ... as if the blue water curved into space beyond the horizon where our pollutants would fall off the edge. French rivers carry 18 billion cubic meters of liquid pollution annually into the sea; Germany's, over 9 billion. The total world production of pesticides was more than 1.4 billion pounds last year. Most of this ultimately finds its way into the ocean. DDT sprayed on crops in East Africa, within a few months, is found in the Bay of Bengal ... a good 4000 miles away! If this continues we will have a dead ocean. And a dead ocean means a dead planet. One can easily see how the Bible's Second Bowl of judgment (where everything in the ocean dies) can soon become a reality. See Revelation 16:3-7.

**Advances
That
Set Us
Backwards**

Now large quantities of toxic nuclear waste are accumulating at atomic power plants. It is becoming a major problem as to where to dump this. By the year 2000 the U.S. military establishment will have produced 11 million cubic feet of nuclear waste. Deadly contamination in the future could kill millions! Is this a man-made Armageddon?

BRAZIL'S "KILLER" BEES: MOVING NORTH STEADILY

RIO DE JANEIRO

Nearly two decades ago, 26 African queen bees and their "families" escaped into the Brazilian countryside from an agricultural experiment station near São Paulo.

The highly productive but vicious insects spread and multiplied throughout most of Brazil's vast territory and into half a dozen adjoining countries. They killed scores of people and thousands of animals.

Now, they may be headed for the United States. Many obstacles lie in their path, but African bees are undaunted by adversity. The question is: How long will it be before they reach Texas, Arizona or California?

African bees are much more aggressive than the familiar European honeybees. They swarm quickly and attack with fury if disturbed by peo-

Killer bee. Officials hope the insect will become tamer as it nears this country.

ple or livestock, or even machines such as tractors and harvesters.

What causes this suicidal frenzy? One Brazilian expert explains: The natives get honey in Africa by burning the hives. Only the hardest bees there survive.

It is this toughness, plus higher

honey production, that led Brazilian authorities in the 1950s to import 36 African queen bees for experiments in crossbreeding with European strains. Crossbred bees, it was believed, would be more docile but as industrious as the "killer" bees.

In 1957, someone accidentally released 26 of the queens which, with their worker and drone followers, fled into the countryside. They've been spreading ever since, even traversing the Amazon jungle.

Tamed in time? The belief here is that they will reach the Southwestern U.S. eventually but will have become much tamer by that time.

Natural crossbreeding with domestic honeybees is said to be making the African invaders gentler but still excellent producers.

As a precaution the U.S. has moved to strengthen its ban on importing honeybees and to step up eradication to control the spread of undesirable species. Yet, experts say the African bee could cross the U.S. border in four to six years or sooner as a stray hitchhiker on a ship or plane.

BIRDS ARE A PLAGUE TO SOUTHERN AFRICA

SALISBURY, Rhodesia (AP)—A two-ounce bird has developed into a modern plague in southern Africa, replacing the locust as the continent's worst problem in nature.

It is the quelea finch, or red-billed quelea — pronounced KWEE-leah. One official estimates that there are 10 quadrillion of them south of the Sahara. That is a thousand times a trillion.

In the last 25 years, the queleas have grown from a nuisance to a major headache, with the help of bigger and better grain crops.

The birds need lots of water and various areas where they existed in naturally controlled numbers are now linked by dams and irrigation projects, making once hazardous migrations much easier.

Queleas once died in vast numbers in the rainy season

Nuclear Fallout Of Chinese Blast Detected in East

By WALTER SULLIVAN

Radioactive fallout from the Chinese nuclear blast 10 days ago has swept across the Pacific Ocean and been detected in eastern Pennsylvania, New Jersey, South Carolina and New York state, including unusually high readings in parts of Long Island and upstate, the Federal Energy Research and Development Administration reported yesterday.

Parched Wales Learns to Live With Drought

By PETER T. KILBORN
Special to The New York Times

CARDIFF, Wales, Sept. 8—The great European drought, the worst in at least 250 years, has drained Britain more than any other country and the area surrounding the Welsh capital of Cardiff more than any other in Britain.

too hard. Cardiff's derelict port has a strong smell because the rivers are not feeding it, and a rent collector said residents of public housing near the port have started complaining about rats.

Despite the assorted effects of the drought, it seems that most people see it first in terms of their toilets. This

Aswan Dam Alters Marine Ecology

By DANA ADAMS SCHMIDT
Special to The New York Times

BEIRUT, Lebanon, June 6 —The salt content and temperature of the eastern Mediterranean are being raised as a result of the building of the Aswan High Dam, according to scientists at the American

pointed out that less water was reaching the Mediterranean from the Nile because more water was evaporating from Lake Nasser the storage reservoir, and from new irrigation works.

We are witnessing an increase in devastating plagues.

**Killer Bee
On the Loose**

About 20 years ago, 26 African queen bees with their worker and drone followers, disappeared into the Brazilian countryside. They had been released accidentally from an experimental station near Sao Paulo.

Though highly productive, they are vicious and are known to have killed scores of people and thousands of animals in Brazil's vast territory. It is expected that these killer bees will reach the U.S. by the late 1980's. It is hoped that natural cross-breeding along the way will soften their aggressiveness. How interesting in light of the Fifth Trumpet judgment of the Tribulation Period when for 5 months people are subjected to the painful stings of a new strain of locusts. See Revelation 9:3-12.

**Too Little Rain
and
Too Much Rain**

In the summer of 1976, Europe suffered one of the worst droughts in history. This was preceded by weeks of scorching sunshine where the temperature hovered in the 90's. Cattle were slaughtered in France and Switzerland because of the lack of fresh grass. The price of hay skyrocketed from $70 a ton to over $125 a ton. Water shortages reduced England to severe rationing. This odd weather, many believe has been caused by the receding of the polar ice cap. The drought in Europe occurred during the same time Russia suffered the worst rains in 100 years, causing shortages of fruit and vegetables.

**Mosquitoes
Linked to
Million Deaths**

Along with this, the National Academy of Sciences say that mosquitoes now contribute to a million deaths annually around the world and the problem will become worse!

CHANGES IN WORLD RESOURCES

11:59

66 If the United States turns completely vegetarian, our agriculture can support 800 million people instead of 200 million. But the world is increasing at 90 million people a year, so that only gives us nine years.

What do you do for an encore after those nine years? 99

William Paddock
Scientist

COUNTDOWN 11:59 TO RAPTURE — FAMINE

America On the Edge

Famine is casting its grim global shadow across the earth and its spectre can even now be seen in the United States. Already, over 20 million Americans must rely on the U.S. Government to provide them with food stamps. It is not uncommon for some Americans to eat dog food.

20% Starving

But this is a banquet compared to how third-world nations live. While about 1.4 billion people can worry about reducing diets ... over 2.5 billion citizens of underdeveloped countries are ill-fed: at least 60% of them are malnourished and 20% more are starving!

Gone are the days of the 1960's which showed bountiful harvests when the United Nation's Food and Agricultural Organization worried about how to dispose of a glut of food. Now the world reserves are at the lowest point since World War 2, amounting to a mere 23 days of consumption. And the margin of safety is decreasing! One big crop failure could mean mass starvation!

Death Toll Staggering

In Africa it is not unusual for 100,000 to die in one season because of famine. Drought is a terrible enemy to Africans but so also is too much rain. Rain washes away topsoil.

In India, half of its 600 million people eat only 1 meal a day ... and that one very meager in nutritional value! The Black Horse of Famine which is already now beginning to sweep the world is a forerunner of the dreaded Third Seal judgment during the Tribulation Period (see Revelation 6:5).

The paradox of life! A grossly distended belly is the final stage prior to death by starvation. Thousands of African children die because they have no food to eat . . . while in America multiple thousands of baby chicks were put in drums and drowned to protest the lack of profits in poultry!

COUNTDOWN
11:59
TO RAPTURE

FAMINE

**30% Die
Before the
Age of 4**

In third world nations malnutrition is the biggest single contributor to infant and young child mortality where 30% die before the age of 4. In rural India about 80% of preschool children suffer from "dwarfism" or stunted growth.

**The Haves
and the
Have Nots**

A conflict between two worlds is developing . . . the rich and the poor. On the rich side are about 24 nations whose 750 million citizens consume most of the world's resources, produce most of its manufactured goods and enjoy history's highest standard of living. On the other side are about 100 underdeveloped nations with over 2 billion people . . . existing under the shadow of death.

**Food
the Big Issue**

In the year 2000 the major issue in presidential politics may be food. In order to meet food requirements worldwide by that year, food production will have to grow by an average of 4% a year. At present this is impossible!

**Energy
and
Weather**

Two problems compound the food dilemma: the energy crisis and changing weather patterns. The cost of fuel is rising and the reserves of oil are rapidly diminishing. Weather has taken a turn for the worse, creating abnormal weather conditions.

**Enter
the
Analog**

Soon Americans will be eating less nutritional-value food and more "analog" foods . . . foods that are similar in looks but not in origin. Soy bean analogs will replace meat. Some have already been found in U.S. supermarkets! American diets will soon be taking a drastic change and not for the better!

11:57

66 ... hamburger and fries at a fast food restaurant have replaced the evening meal for many families. That's the one meal when the whole family sits down together and interacts, and it's very important in keeping the family together.

Without the necessary interaction of the mother and father and children you have families breaking up. And any number of health problems can be traced to the breakdown of the family. 99

Dr. Leonard Bachman
Pennsylvania Health Secretary

COUNTDOWN 11:57 TO RAPTURE · FOOD

Having it Your Way May Not Be the Best Way!

Americans are eating the wrong foods, hollow foods that offer little in nutrition and include a host of questionable additives. The result: many more are prone to illness, an inability to concentrate, a growing restlessness and disturbances of the mind.

In the early 1950's only a few cents out of the average family food dollar went for meals away from home. Today the figure is 40¢. By 1980 it will be 50¢. Food service is the third largest consumer industry. This year's sales surpass $70 billion. There are over 500,000 fast food restaurants. McDonald's, as an example, sells one billion hamburgers every four months requiring 100,000 head of cattle. One University of Illinois professor calculated that the napkins, hamburger boxes, bags and cups for one year's use in McDonald's eats up annually the sustained yield of more than 630 square miles of forest.

Fast food chains spend over $275 million to attract customers. And about 95% of this budget will go for TV advertising.

"Bug-Burgers"

Meanwhile research is being done on the value of eating insects should a food shortage develop. Could we one day be eating "bug-burgers?" A University of Wisconsin entomology professor says: "Termites have a higher protein content than beef or fish." In some countries locusts are the "french fries." The food crisis may one day force Americans to sit down to a salad of creepy crawlers.

Today more than 75% of the items stocked by supermarkets bear the UPC (Uniform Pricing Code) symbol. See inset. Pictured is a computerized scanning system that will soon be in supermarkets nationwide.

The Dangerous Trend of Farming

There is an agricultural revolution going on in the United States. Food control is passing into the hands of a few.

The number of farms in the U.S. has declined from 5.6 million in 1950 to 2.2 million in 1980. Last year for every 70 Americans, there was one farmer. Small farmers are finding it just about impossible to exist. They are forced to sell out to large corporation-combines. More and more the food of the nation is in the hands of a few; a few who can control the output and price of the food you eat tomorrow!

The Tightening Control of Food Production

There are some 32,000 food manufacturing firms in the U.S., but just 50 of these companies make about three-quarters of the industry's profits. Author Jim Hightower alleges that "Wheaties cost around 93¢ for a regular size box. Yet there is no more than two cents worth of wheat in Wheaties; the box costs more than that. Total is Wheaties plus a half-cent worth of vitamins sprayed on, but it is sold for 22 cents more."

The Increasing Dependence on the Government

In 1965, just 632,000 Americans were receiving food stamps, depending on the U.S. Government to feed them. By 1980 this had risen to over 20 million! Former Agriculture Secretary, Earl L. Butz, commented, "In the long run, agripower has to be more important than petropower." This will be prophetically true as food becomes the ultimate weapon in world politics. Revelation 13:16-18 reveals that in the Tribulation Period no man will be able to buy or sell without the Mark of Antichrist.

11:55

66 We must reduce the birthrate and lower the population, but that will take time. What do we do meanwhile?

We must ... move on to new lands. Since there are no new lands on earth worth the taking, we must move to new worlds and colonize the heavens. 99

Isaac Asimov
Scientist

World Population Past 4 Billion Mark

Although some would rather ignore and explain away the threat of a world population explosion . . . nevertheless, it still does pose a major problem in the ensuing years. Abortion and sterilization are not the answer.

On March 28, 1976, the world population was clocked speeding past the 4 billion mark. It should double that in 38-40 years! Some people believe that acquiring new lands in outer space is the only answer to finally solve the population crisis.

Inhabiting Outer Space

Some suggest placing hollow cylinders in space half-way between the earth and moon. Astronomer Joseph Louis Lagrange, in 1772, suggested that such a position for space cylinders would be ideal. The competing gravities of earth and moon would keep the life-supporting cylinders in place. Sunshine, reflected by long mirrors would provide daylight and a night and day atmosphere could be achieved.

The inner surface of the opaque portions of the cylinder would be spread with soil. This could be used for agriculture and even animal husbandry. Two cylinders of this nature, one writer suggests, could support 10,000 people. Cylinders as wide as Manhattan and half again as long could support up to 20 million people. On this present earth, we add about 200,000 inhabitants every day! It is quite possible within the next 30 years . . . what was considered science fiction, may one day become a reality!

45

What does the
population explosion
have to do with...

inflation? . . . . When more and more people compete to buy limited goods or resources, prices go up. That's a basic reason for inflation, though the whole story is more complicated.

energy crisis? . . . When more and more people compete to buy more and more energy, the price climbs and shortages are further aggravated.

food shortages? . With 75 million additional people every year pressing against limited world food resources, shortages, higher prices, and famine are as certain as the setting of the sun.

lack of housing? When more people compete for housing, then mortgage rates, land costs, and construction prices all move upward. And decent housing moves further out of reach for an increasing number of people.

Some people will quarrel with these explanations as over-simplified. Of course they are; little in life is uncomplicated. But no one should quarrel with this truth: If our globe had fewer people on it, most of its problems would find easier solutions, and the quality of life for all would be improved.

So won't you help the Population Institute's campaign to *motivate* all potential parents to reduce their childbearing? We're doing that around the world by enlisting the aid of those national and world organizations that, through the creative impact of entertainers, writers, journalists, editors, broadcasters, publishers, teachers, clergy, statesmen, and activists, can reach out again and again to the people of the world with the message that . . .

whatever your cause, it's a lost cause unless we halt the population explosion

You can help solve the population crisis by sending a check today to: The Population Institute, 100 Maryland Ave., N.E., Washington, D.C. 20002

The Population Institute
100 Maryland Avenue, N.E.
Washington, D.C. 20002

I am glad to invest in the Population Institute's continuing campaign to improve the quality of life by checking the population explosion. I enclose: $............

NAME: ....

ADDRESS: ....

.... ZIP ....

(Contributions are tax deductible)

You will see more full page ads like these designed to limit population growth. One day birth control will become compulsary.

COUNTDOWN 11:55 TO RAPTURE | **POPULATION EXPLOSION**

Runaway Population Growth

Many people are unaware just how rapidly the population is exploding. It took all of recorded history for the world to produce its first billion inhabitants around 1850!

Then 80 years were needed to pass the 2 billion mark in 1930, and another 31 years to reach 3 billion in 1961.

But only 15 years were required to add the 4th billion in 1976. (5 billion will be reached in 13 years!)

The U.S. growth rate is 0.8% annually. The world average is 1.9% because such countries as Mexico and third world nations have as high as 3.5% annual growth rate. As an example, on the average, a new classroom is built in Mexico every 50 minutes. But during this same short time 246 new children are born.

Gloomy Future Forecast

Some believe population explosion brings with it inflation as more and more people compete to buy limited goods. Housing and food become major economic problems worldwide. Side effects such as the financial breakdown of New York City and increased drug use among youth are population explosion related.

In October, 1975, some 400 scientists, scholars, businessmen and political leaders met in Houston, Texas to ponder the problems facing mankind. They predicted a gloomy future for the world . . . bankrupt cities, dire food shortages, a catastrophic breakdown of society and unprecedented wars.

Forced Sterilization Slated
To Curb India's Population

By KAI BIRD
Chicago Daily News

New Delhi, April 10 — India soon will become the first nation to practice forced sterilizations.

In an effort to face up to the country's overpopulation problem, the government of Prime Minister Indira Gandhi is encouraging local authorities to legislate compulsory sterilizations. The first such measure is expected to become effective by the end of the year in the densely populated but fertile state of Punjab. Under the pending new law there, any couple having a third child will face either one year in prison and a $250 fine or mandatory sterilization.

be required to undergo sterilization. Parents of handicapped children also would be exempt.

The legislature of Maharashtra State last week approved a compulsory sterilization law which would take effect if a family has had three children. The measure was sent to the president of India for expected approval.

Another state, West Bengal, is drafting sterilization legislation.

The capital principality of Delhi has enacted a law which acts against government employes with more than two children. The municipal law states that no one can be hired by the civil administration who has more than two children. Municipal housing will not be available to civil servants who have more than two children.

A number of different measures are under consideration by other state governments. But most states will refrain from actually enforcing their new population control measures until the federal government unveils a national law.

Mrs. Gandhi Confirms Some Died
In Protests Over Sterilization Drive

NEW DELHI, Oct. 27—Prime Minister Indira Gandhi disclosed today that some people had been killed in clashes with the police growing out of India's campaign of mass sterilization.

In a speech in Parliament, the Prime Minister confirmed reccurring rumors of rioting by people protesting the sterilization program, which many say is the most vigorous in the country's history. But she gave no details.

not abiding by the directions of the Prime Minister."

Today Mr. Sait and six other opposition Members of Parliament drove to Muzaffarnagar, 50 miles north of here, and came back with an estimate that several dozen people had been killed and 150 wounded in incidents earlier this month.

The group of lawmakers reported that after talking to some local residents they had been turned away by local police

What has happened in India can also happen here.

COUNTDOWN 11:55 TO RAPTURE POPULATION EXPLOSION

Life Expectancy Increases and Compounds Population Explosion Fears

Nine out of 10 people added to the earth's population will be in the poorer, underdeveloped nations. These are countries where feeding billions of people is already proving a near-insurmountable challenge. Crowded conditions produce violence ... and violence, war. While the world's birth rate is on a small decline ... the death rates have changed as medical advances have increased life expectancy by 20 years. In less than 100 years the world population is expected to hit 12 billion people.

Rising Elderly Population

The elderly population in the United States has grown by 2.4 million since 1970. There are now over 23 million elderly.

Breeding Grounds for Rise of Antichrist

One answer to exploding population will be the loss of freedoms. There will be a greater spread of authoritarian governments ... an excellent breeding ground for Antichrist!

Forced Sterilization Coming

In September, 1976 a record 1.3 million persons were sterilized in India, bringing the total to 3.4 million in the previous six months. India adds more than one million in new births each month and has a population of over 620 million! Some widespread riots have occurred in India over rumors of forcible sterilizations. Many have been killed in these riots. Soon India will institute a program of forced sterilization. She will become the first country to do so. But others will follow. And eventually, perhaps even the United States!

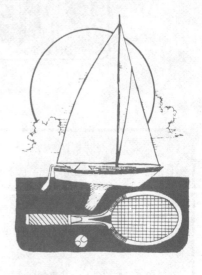

CHANGES
IN
VALUES

11:58

66 Many a man thinks he is buying pleasure, when he is really selling himself a slave to it.

Benjamin Franklin

. . . she that liveth in pleasure is dead while she liveth.

1 Timothy 5:6

He that loveth pleasure shall be a poor man; he that loveth wine and oil shall not be rich. 99

Proverbs 21:17

The Million Dollar Stars

In June, 1976, Bobby Orr became a superstar when the Chicago Black Hawks, an ice hockey team, offered him a $2.8 million unconditional contract . . . just another in the escalating salaries paid sports and motion picture stars.

And in the news reporting field, Barbara Walters was successful in securing a $1 million contract to switch networks.

$600 Monthly For a Manicurist

Meanwhile advertisers are willing to pay $70,000 a minute to be included in the Sonny and Cher TV specials. One writer alleges that Cher each month spends $6000 for clothes, $900 for a psychiatrist and $600 for her manicurist, while living in a $2 million Beverly Hills home.

In that same year, 1976, Elvis Presley performed to his largest audience, 60,000 fans, in Pontiac, Michigan. The crowd paid almost $1 million to see him!

Millions in Profits at $4 a Ticket

The motion picture **JAWS** outdid **THE GODFATHER.** THE GODFATHER, released in 1972, has grossed over $90 million in domestic rentals, while JAWS, in less than 90 days grossed over $100 million. JAWS cost $8 million to make and about $2 million to promote.

Universal Studios, **JAWS'** production company, may clear $60 million alone! Within its first 24 days of release the film took in nearly $50 million! Worldwide distribution of the film will probably generate over $200 million!

You are looking at $1 million in cash! It is not unusual for baseball players to receive $2 to $3 million in guaranteed contracts!

Olympics, The Big Business of Sports

In 776 B.C. on the plain of Olympia beside the Alpheus River in Greece, the Olympic games were started.

By A.D. 394 the Roman Emperor Theodosius abolished the games because of growing evidence of cheating and using the games for political gain. They were later reinstated.

The 1976 summer Olympics in Canada were a prime example of political maneuver. It was here that Canada's leader, Mr. Trudeau, yielded to mainland China's pressure and barred Free China from participating in the Olympics under her own flag. The reason: Red China's mammoth purchases of Canadian wheat!

Sports and particularly the Olympics have become big business. ABC bid $25 million for the privilege of telecasting the Montreal Olympics in 1976. This was **twice** the amount paid for these events in 1972. TV rights for the 1980 Olympics are expected to go for $50 million!

Revenues from the sale of commercials came to over $40 million.

200 Pairs of Shoes

Between 4-year Olympics, the $3 billion annual music olympics fills in. Singers like Elton John have been responsible for over 42 million album sales which bring him (along with personal appearances) an estimated $7 million in annual income. He allegedly has an eyeglass collection worth over $40,000 and some 200 pairs of shoes. And people actually pay to hear albums such as *Captain Fantastic and the Dirt Brown Cowboy!*

MONTREAL OLYMPICS : 16000 MAN
SECURITY FORCE FOR 12000 ATHLETES.

In the 1908 Olympics in London, expenditures for "equipment, police supervision and messengers" came to less than $5,000. In the 1976 Olympics in Montreal, "supervision" cost well over $100 million! This made Montreal Olympics the most expensive security operation in history. Security averaged $8000 per athlete! All this was needed to prevent a terrorist attack!

**How the
Love of Money
Spawns Evil**

The American Dream has become a nightmare. And many of the States are trying to outdo themselves in offering the most lucrative-looking lotteries to their residents.

The get-rich-quick idea is shouted from the television screen and saturated through billboard coverage.

Distribution is the key and almost any store can be the "entrance to eternal joy" where one can purchase a lottery ticket.

Not satisfied with lottery sales where it takes a week or a month to see who the winner is . . . they now have gone one better . . . the INSTANT LOTTERY. Buy a ticket . . . presto! You can tell immediately if you've won or lost.

**Gambling
Now a
Way of Life**

Soon Las Vegas will not be the only spot where one can gamble . . . the East Coast is not to be outdone and Atlantic City may eventually become the gambling counterpart of Vegas.

In Las Vegas $4 million crosses the gaming tables every weekend!

"Legalize gambling," many respected leaders suggest. They try to convince the unwary public that legalization will deter crime and give the state more money. But many states have already discovered the folly of such thinking . . . so what do they do . . . they make the prizes bigger. Now you can become a MILLIONAIRE in the Million Dollar lotteries! Where will it end? At Armageddon!

11:55

66 We all keep hoping each night we meet that this will be
the last time we have to do this. 99
> Teacher volunteer
> holding "underground school."

Underground Schools . . . a Sign of Things to Come?

For over 8 weeks in a suburban community north of Philadelphia the Centennial School District teacher's strike droned on. It began in September, 1976. It was now the end of October. Parents were getting frantic. Suddenly "underground" schools began to crop up. Classrooms were held in kitchens. The Huntingdon Valley Methodist Church opened its doors for math classes for 93 elementary school students. "Underground" classes were being held at McDonald's restaurant in Southampton. Mothers pitched in to teach. Teachers were in a striking mood and every September sees an increasing number of teacher strikes that seem to last longer and longer. In desperation, students conduct rallies deploring teacher strikes and their right as a student to get an education. In the last year there were some 60 teacher strikes affecting more than 2.5 million students.

The Big Squeeze Is On

Schools are coming into hard times. The worst money squeeze in years is producing big cutbacks in classrooms. There are fewer teachers, fewer sports, shabbier surroundings. And teacher strikes compound the money problems, local community action rebels against high school taxes and the end result is an austere school program.

The Day Money Runs Out

Employee pay and benefits consume 75% of school budgets. In one year, New York City lost 12,000 teachers through layoffs or attrition. Summer schools have been eliminated in some communities. Soon quality education will be a thing of the past.

Los Angeles teacher wears a wrist transmitter. If trouble develops, she pushes a button which transmits an alarm, bringing in a security guard.

"THIRD ASSAULT TODAY—JUST ABOUT NORMAL
FOR A USUAL SCHOOL DAY."

**College
Students
That
Can't Spell**

Nationwide, the statistics on literacy grow more appalling each year. Erosion in reading skills among American students began in 1965. Colleges and universities are finding that many freshman can't organize their thoughts on paper, and make simple spelling errors. At the University of California (where students come from the top 12% of high-school graduates), nearly half demonstrated writing skills so poor that they had to enroll in remedial catch-up courses! A seemingly endless procession of poor scores in national testing programs is raising fresh doubts about the kind of education our youngsters are getting in today's American public schools.

**Dropouts
Increasing**

Another concern is school dropouts and pushouts. At any given time there are 2.4 million young Americans between 7 and 19 who do not attend school.

**School
Violence
a $30 Million
Tragedy**

Some get in trouble. Violence and vandalism in the nation's public schools are approaching epidemic proportions. Nobody seems to know what to do about it! In just 3 years between 1973 and 1976: school-related homicides increased by 18%; rapes and attempted rapes by 40%; robberies up 37%; assault on students soared up to 85% and assaults on teachers went up 77%. In New York police must grapple with 350 youth gangs. In Chicago a budget of $10 million must be allocated just to stabilize disorder in schools! In Dade County (Miami), Florida, attacks on teachers and administrators totaled 225 last year! A Gallup poll of adults believe the problem is: lack of discipline!

61

11:58

66 They don't know what's coming up in the future — and their morales need a boost. 99
> New York Furrier
> Commenting on the sale
> of $23,000 Russian-sable coats

For the Man Who Has Everything

Rolls-Royce's $33,500 Silver Shadow sedan has been selling so well that the company is offering it as a part of its new line of Christmas gift certificates. In Boston, the doors of one furrier had to be locked several times a day just so salesmen could deal with the customers already inside!

In Cartier's on New York's Fifth Avenue it is not unusual for 30 of their $750 watches to be purchased daily. And *Town & Country* carries ads for $75,000 sable coats. In 1975, 1250 passengers plunked down $10,000 a piece for a round-the-world trip on Cunard's Queen Elizabeth 2, guzzling down 17,100 bottles of champagne and wine in 80 days of leisure.

Millionaires On the Increase

While 1948 witnessed only 13,000 millionaires in the U.S.; in 1976 there were over 240,000 (1 out of every 900 Americans).

To capture this wealth Sunday retailing has become a way of life with more and more stores opening on Sunday.

Back to the Days of Rome

Americans are becoming more sports minded. Thomas Jefferson bought Louisiana in 1803 for $15 million. But the Superdome in New Orleans cost $163 million! Over 21 superdomes have already been built in the U.S. Gambling, once condemned, is now taking on a new air of official acceptance. A growing number of states have put their stamp of approval on gambling. Some 15 states have lotteries and there is every indication that more states will enter the frantic race to capture the gambling dollar in the name of charity.

Big Stores Joining in Sunday Retailing

By ISADORE BARMASH

Sunday shopping on a mass basis came to New York City and the metropolitan area yesterday when four of the largest retailers opened their doors, most of them for th... fi...

but two other Macy's stores in the city—in the Kings Plaza Shopping Center and on Staten Island—were open, as were 10 other Macy's stores in the state.

Perhaps 100 shoppers waited ...cy's Herald Squa... noon yesterday, ... doors to be op... ...ey drifted over... Gimbels and ... which were ... e big retailers ...tion with the ...esman for ... was sligh... ...ur two prev...

...Chasanoff, g... the Gimb... ...et and Br... pleased—i... urday."

...th Siegel, ... Macy's i... "Busin... antici... ...ertz st... ...hing, ...

day," said Heywood Wilansky, group merchandise manager.

Korvettes' open doors also attracted an arsonist. Firemen were called shortly after 4 P.M. when a fire was discovered in a publio area of the ... in the store on ...

One can easily see how the "Eat, drink and be merry" philosophy is increasing in these Last Days.

COUNTDOWN **11:58** TO RAPTURE — **MODERN LIVING**

The Agony of Boredom

Americans are restless. That's why a large crowd gathered to watch 22,222 dominoes topple. The domino maze covered 121 square yards of the University of Pennsylvania's dormitory and took 19 hours to set up. It took 8-minutes, 30 seconds for the dominoes to topple.

Some 8000 motorcyclists merged on the Pennsylvania state capitol protesting the state law requiring them to wear helmets (one cyclist was thrown off his bike in a collision with an automobile!). People's senses dulled by too many amusements; their energies dissipated over insignificant non-essentials . . . this is some of the harvest of modern living.

The Age of Throwaway Marriages

We are living in the age of "throwaway marriages." Continuing the trend of recent years, divorces among Americans in 1975 exceeded a million for the first time, while the number of marriages declined significantly. The number of single women in 1976 between the age of 20 to 24 is 40%. In 1960 it was only 28%. Today it is estimated that 1 marriage out of 4 ends in divorce. And in 80% of the cases, both partners will remarry. Counselors acknowledge that divorce is a major factor in contributing to juvenile delinquency.

The Tragedy of Old Age

About two-thirds of every federal dollar spent on health care goes to America's 22 million senior citizens. Yet one-third of them are below or hover above the poverty line. And 25% of all suicides in the U.S. are committed by people over 65.

11:57

66 SPLIT LOGS — NOT ATOMS

TAKE A TREE TO LUNCH **99**

Signs on Bumper Stickers

Seeking a Quiet Lifestyle

Lifestyles seem to be changing. Many young people (and adults, too), tired of the pressure cooker atmosphere of making a living, are going to the remaining wide open spaces and getting back to nature.

Struggling To Reach the Top

But for every one who is fed up with the rat race of 20th century civilization, there are countless others still striving to make it to the top in their field. Money is used to buy influence to get into medical school; suddenly West Point and Annapolis are plagued by students who cheat on exams. In the business field, bribes into the millions are used to capture contracts worldwide. College degrees now appear meaningless as college graduates, who can't get jobs in their field of training, go to pumping gas or waiting on tables. In 1790 only 5% of Americans lived in urban areas. Today almost 80% live in urban areas. In 1800 each woman of childbearing age had about 7 children; today it is less than 2.

A Shift in Occupations

In 1870, 24 out of every 100 people in the U.S. were farmers (as were 24 women out of every 100). Today only 3 out of every 100 men are farmers. In 1870 only 1 out of 100 were retired. Today 9 out of every 100 is either retired or disabled. In 1830 only 4% were 60 or over; today it is 15%. Television, amusements, sports, have warped our priorities and the unity of the home has become something one reads about in old-fashioned stories. We have become automatons living life for today and caring little about tomorrow.

A Shift in Priorities

CHANGES
IN
QUALITY
OF LIFE

11:58

66 At the suggestion of a marketing consultant, the banks gave the program a name that didn't suggest computers (*Apex* was chosen). Also, the banks agreed to concentrate on electronic payroll *deposits* rather than bill *payments*. 'It was easier to tell the public we're facilitating money going into their accounts rather than facilitating money going out,' recalls Virgil M. Dismeyer, senior vice-president for Northwestern National Bank.

In some ways, the strategies have paid off. Apex now claims more private-industry users than any other automated clearing house.

> Joann S. Lublin
> Staff Reporter
> The Wall Street Journal

And he (the false prophet) causeth all, both small and great, rich and poor, free and enslaved, to receive a mark in their right hand, or in their foreheads.

And that no man might buy or sell, except he that had the mark, or the name of the beast (antichrist), or the number of his name (666). 99

> Revelation 13:16, 17

COUNTDOWN 11:58 TO RAPTURE — COMPUTERS

The Microcomputer Is Born

This is not only the age of the computer but also the age of the microcomputer.

The microcomputer industry is now capturing a billion-dollar market. The father is the computer, the son is the minicomputer, and now the baby in the industry is the microcomputer. The incredible microcomputer can communicate with an infinite number of devices and is comparatively inexpensive.

Checks Are Out of Style

The computer is encouraging many businesses to do "checkless" banking by way of electronic funds transfer systems. Already, remote banking terminals that let customers make withdrawals with a "cash card" are fixtures in many shopping centers.

About 700 companies, local governments and institutions offer checkless payroll and bill-paying services.

Pay By Telephone

Some savings banks are setting up systems where individuals can pay bills by telephone. No checks, no signatures, no postage stamps!

Computer Control Means Power

Computerized markings on food products will soon generate a new way of buying without cash! Today, there are over 500,000 computers in operation in the United States. By manipulating a computer, a teller at New York's Dime Savings Bank was able to embezzle $1.4 million over a 3 year period. **Whoever can control the computer can control human life!**

11:59

66 The problem of serious crime is immense . . . a national problem. . . .

Attorney General Edward H. Levi

America has been far from successful in dealing with the sort of crime that obsesses Americans day and night — street crime, crime that invades our neighborhoods and our homes . . . brutal violence that makes us fearful of strangers and afraid to go out at night. 99

Gerald Ford, President, 1973-76

The Runaway Crime Rate

Since 1961 the rate for all serious crimes has more than doubled. Last year it jumped almost 20% — the largest increase in the 46 years that national statistics have been collected.

Violent crime has had an even sharper increase. In the past 14 years, the rate of robberies has increased 255%, forcible rape 143% and murder 106%.

The rate of increase of crime in the suburbs has surpassed that of the cities (up 20% last year) and in rural areas (up 21%). About 70% of all adults imprisoned for serious crime are repeaters who have already been in jail at least once before.

Are We Reaping What We Deserve?

Old values and morals went down the drain in the early 1960's and America is now reaping the harvest of the wild seed it has sown. The 19th century French criminologist Jean Lacassagne said: "A Society gets the criminals it deserves."

In 1980 alone, criminals killed more than 22,000 people and stole property worth over $3 billion!

They Even Steal Bibles!

The combined cost of shoplifting, employee theft and hijacking is running well above $25 billion a year! An estimated 4580 Bibles were stolen from New York hotel rooms in one year! Prison populations are expected to grow by 50% in the next 5 years!

An elderly woman, on her way to the Flower Mart in downtown Baltimore, is manhandled by protesting youths.

COUNTDOWN 11:59 TO RAPTURE   CRIME

Juvenile Crime Soaring

Juvenile crime has risen by 1600% in the last 20 years. This statistic is awesome! What is breaking down the American family? The new morality? Yes. The advance of fast-food fare restaurants which encourage little family communication? Yes. The school systems that omit the Bible and a Biblical standard of discipline? Yes.

Juvenile crime costs the United States over $12 billion annually. Nationally, about 2975 juvenile courts and 3,202 judges hear approximately a million cases a year.

Crime Wave Hits Churches

Suddenly even people in churches find themselves victims of the crime wave. Clergymen find it necessary to hire guards, to protect the parking lots and the offering. Doors of the church are bolted during the service. Last year nearly 2500 crimes of all types were committed against houses of worship in New York City alone!

Bodyguards are becoming a big business. By 1980, 70,000 bodyguards will be employed to guard American businessmen and celebrities.

Group 666

In July, 1976, twenty-six children and their bus driver were kidnapped in a mass abduction. Nothing is sacred anymore with the criminal. In Grenoble, France, October, 1976, a young man and woman were found murdered by a hitherto unheard-of organization calling itself, "Group 666 of the Red Brigade."

11:56

66 Article 36 of the Statute of the Court, by providing for compulsory jurisdiction, offers a way by which more issues could be brought before the Court for resolution by judicial means. 99

Kurt Waldheim
Secretary-General, UN

The Coming World Law

The obsession with world law is becoming greater and greater in the United Nations. Third World nations are increasing in their power and influence.

While on one hand, in the United States, we are having breakdown of law and order . . . on the other hand more countries are accepting a dictatorial-type of government in order to maintain a semblance of order. They accept a repressive society.

A Desire to Détente

And the United States continues to recognize such countries, and (as in the Helsinki agreement) is willing to offer up free countries as pawns to Russia in order to maintain some type of détente.

Compulsory World Law An Eventuality

More and more the United Nations is pushing for a world order (as are some intellectual-type Americans). They see this as a cure-all for the world's ills . . . suggesting that the United States forget its nationalism and submit to a higher world order . . . a world government that would transcend natural boundaries.

The United Nations would like to see its International Court of Justice exercise a compulsory jurisdiction over its members. Article 36 of the UN is aimed at this eventuality. At present only 45 of the Membership have accepted this compulsory jurisdiction. This is less than 1/4th. But world control is a coming eventuality.

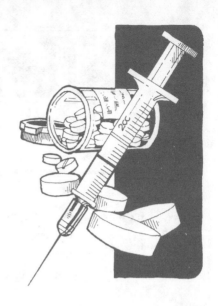

CHANGES
IN
HEALTH
CARE

11:55

66 We don't know what we're dealing with . . . we have not seen anything like this take place in such a short period of time. 99

Dr. Leonard C. Bachman
Pennsylvania Health Secretary
in reference to "Legionaire's Disease"

**Mystery
Ailments
Increasing**

It was to be a gala celebration. The American Legion was meeting at the Bellevue Stratford Hotel for its July, 1976 convention. But just a few weeks later . . . within a 6 day period . . . 29 people mysteriously died. And still no one really knows the cause! The Bellevue Stratford was forced to close its doors.

In October, 1976, when the first breeze of autumn turned the summer's lush greenery to brown, a Kittaning, Pennsylvania electronics plant shut down when 242 of its 289 workers were hospitalized in a mysterious illness.

**Even
Mothers' Milk
Unsafe**

Recently the American Medical Society along with the Food and Drug Administration have become concerned with PCB (polychlorinated biphenyls). PCB is a colorless and tasteless compound used in industry. A recent study revealed that PCB was found in the milk of mothers tested in 11 states at levels considered unsafe. Now, even mothers' milk is contaminated!

**Growing
Misuse of
Drugs
Cause Death**

The growing use and misuse of drugs is having its effect on the U.S. population. Valium, the popular tranquilizer, is prescribed 5 million times a month in the U.S.; Librium, 1.5 million a month! The FDA has warned that such drugs may cause birth defects. *The Journal of American Medicine* in its August 9, 1976 issue reports: "Not only is the percentage of deaths that occur in Adverse Drug Reactions not accurately known, but the actual number of nationwide deaths from ADRs is also unknown . . . estimates (of deaths) range from 300 to 140,000 per year."

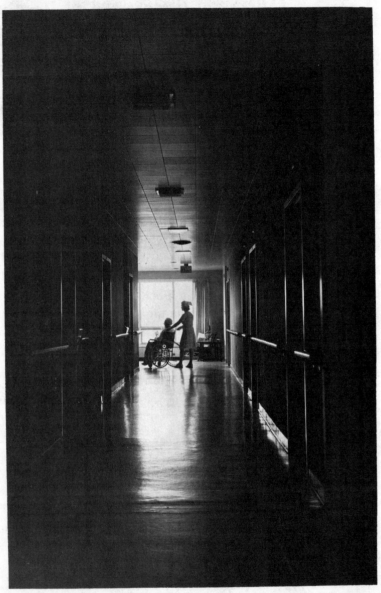

Average hospital visit in 1965 was $300. Today it is almost $2000!

Multiple Cancers Increasing

Multiple cancers are on the increase. Those having breast cancer face an increased risk of later developing ovarian cancer, and vice versa. Those who submit to radiation therapy sometimes develop radiation-caused cancers five or more years later. Doctors are still seeking the cause of cancer. Unorthodox approaches, such as those used by Dr. Carey Reams, believe it to be related to a mineral deficiency. The use of drugs appears to extend life somewhat but unleashes a host of side effects.

Medicaid Abuse Rampant

Medicaid, with a budget of over $3 billion, is rampant with fraud and abuse. A Senate investigating staff found in New York State alone $444 million is lost annually through Medicaid fraud. In one clinic an investigator was told her urine was normal "... even though it was soap and a cleaner combination the investigator had concocted in the rest room."

The Penalty of Progress

Child abuse is reaching frightening proportions. It is estimated that some 60,000 to 70,000 children annually are victims of the "battered child syndrome." Parents, living in a fast-moving world, struggling for existence, find themselves short-tempered, ill, and take it out on their children. Depression accounts for 75% of all psychiatric hospitalizations. It is estimated that some 20% of the U.S. population suffers from chronic depression. While the world has advanced technologically, it has done so at the expense of the human being. His ailments are becoming more complex, more mysterious, more deadly.

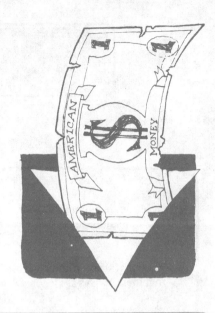

CHANGES
IN
THE
ECONOMY

11:56

66 How much better is it to get wisdom than gold! And to get understanding is rather to be chosen than silver.

Proverbs 16:16

They that trust in their wealth . . . their inward thought is that their houses shall continue forever, and their dwelling places to all generations. . . . 99

Psalms 49:6, 11

$1000 a Week

Pipeline workers in Alaska were earning $1000 to $1500 a week. Garbage collectors in San Francisco are earning $20,000 a year. Yet school teachers struggle to earn $12,000 a year ... some even accepting government food stamps. Pay scale inequalities have generated and will generate more and more strikes which, in turn, will produce higher prices for goods and poorer quality.

Unprofitable Dirt

Farmers, blessed with the richest of soils, can't make a profit on their land. Many work on their land during the day and hold down a factory job at night ... just to keep from going under. A $6000 tractor in 1969 now costs almost $20,000! Small farmers are forced to sell to large corporate combines. Thus the food market is controlled by a select few. The preservatives they put in their food products, the additives and chemical cocktails they combine for greater profit cannot be controlled by the consumer. He becomes a helpless pawn in the battle for the dollar.

The Power Makers

Global corporations now have the power to shape our lives. There is every reason to believe that multi-national corporations will supplant the nation-state as the most powerful force in our lives.

The Coming Controller

Excessive federal spending, along with the failure of government to check inflation, will one day cause chaos and open the door for a benevolent dictatorship in the United States.

'Checkless Society' Takes a Step Closer

By LEONARD SLOANE
N. Y. Times News Service

New York — The "Checkless Society" long a computer man's dream, has been moving closer to development in recent years with the introduction of new processes.

One process is the Pay By Phone system instituted last fall by two savings banks. Customers who open special accounts can call in their payments to cooperating merchants, utilities and other organizations through these

banks — without writing a check or a negotiated order of withdrawal.

Approval Needed

Approval of state banking departments is necessary before such a system can be put into effect. Pay By Phone has been approved by regula-

total and informs the customer of the amount of money left in the account.

Computer Setup

A daily printout is sent to every payee listing the name, account number and amount paid by every payer — along with a single check for the

This is done by first depressing a special number for each of the approximately 300 participating companies — every depositor has a different number for the payees involved as another guard against fraud — and then the amount to be paid.

tion form every month. The banks also benefit from the funds placed in the pay by phone accounts — the average is $1,800 in Minneapolis and $250 in Bridgeport—that might have been in a commercial bank checking account instead.

Computerized Bureaucracy Menaces Privacy, Report Warns

Washington Star

Washington — A White House advisory office says the Government is rushing headlong into using sophisticated electronic systems to move toward a cashless society, without stopping to consider the effects of such a move on individuals' right to privacy.

"Central noneconomic issues have not been ...

port by Prof. James D. Rule, a sociologist at the State University of New York, expressing his concern over how the nation's bureaucracy might make use of the vast bank of personal data that could be collected by a nationwide network of computerized financial information.

Making the assumption that use of electronics to transfer funds and determine con...

and movements to that same purpose," he says.

Rule says valid questions about the way in which such systems are to be developed have not been answered. How much access should the Government be granted to such systems? Should the courts be able to use EFTS to automatically deduct from individual accounts to alimony ...

the record of each transaction would have to identify the parties, including the agency at which the transaction took place.

"The record would also have to include the amount and nature of the transaction, the date, and probably

along the kind of goods or services rendered ... even this much data would obviously be volatile in its personal effects on the user."

In the extreme case of a world blanketed with EFT computer terminals "where all of everyone's con-

sumer transactions took through that medium, EFT would become so automated ... it ... maximum ... activities, as well as his annual resources."

Superbusiness power
Coming conquest of the world

By Richard J. Barnet
and Ronald E. Muller

THE MEN WHO run the global corporations are the first in history with the organization, technology, money, and ideology to make a credible try at managing the world as an integrated unit.

The global visionary of earlier days was either a self-deceiver or a mystic. When Alexander the Great wept by the riverbank because there were no more worlds to conquer, his distress rested on nothing more substantial than the ignorance of his mapmaker. As the boundaries of the known world expanded, a succession of kings, generals, and assorted strong men tried to establish empires of ever more colossal scale, but none succeeded in making a lasting public reality out of private fantasies.

The managers of the world's corporate giants proclaim their faith that where conquest has failed, business can succeed. "In the '40s Wendell Willkie spoke about 'One World,'" says I. B. M. senior vice president Jacques G. Mai...

Planet Earth Inc.

governments on where people live; what work, if any, they will do; what they will eat, drink, and wear; what sorts of knowledge schools and universities will encourage; and what kind of society their children will inherit.

Indeed, the most revolutionary aspect of the planetary enterprise is not its size but its world view. The managers of the global corporations are seeking to put into practice a theory of human organization that will profoundly alter the nation-state system around which society has been organized for over 400 years.

The power of the global corporation derives from its unique capacity to use finance, technology, and advanced marketing skills to integrate production on a worldwide scale and thus to realize the ancient capitalist dream of One Great Market. This cosmopolitan vision stands as a direct challenge to traditional nationalism.

"The political boundaries of nation-states," declares William I. Spencer, president of the First National City Corp., which does business in over 90 ...

Over $1 billion has been invested in 225,000 point-of-sale electronic terminals in stores across the country. The age of the Mark is here!

The Squeeze Is On

An inflationary and power spiral that has no end! That's the situation we are facing.

The energy industry had a total capitalization of $40 billion in 1960. Today it is over $200 billion. And by 1985 their capital requirements will run over $900 billion! They, as well as other industries, find themselves underinvested and overborrowed. The big squeeze is on.

To Exist Is To Be Big

Existence depends on bigness and bigness comes through companies combining their assets. They then become conglomerates and conglomerates become multi-national, joining hands with large conglomerates in other nations. The most successful global corporations boast annual sales that exceed the national income of most countries. And their average growth rate is two to three times that of the most advanced industrial countries, including the United States!

Industry Controls The World

Thus the conglomerate multi-nationals become the first institution in human history dedicated to centralized planning on a world scale.

"A global economy," says John J. Powers, president of Pfizer, "is no idealistic pipe dream but a hard-headed prediction: it is a role into which we are being pushed by the imperatives of our own technology."

And Antichrist Will Control Industry

William I. Spencer, president of First National City Corp. remarks: "The political boundaries of nation-states are too narrow and constricted to define the scope of modern business."

11:59

“ The Federal Reserve (privately owned banks) are one of the most corrupt institutions the world has ever seen.
> Senator Louis T. McFadden
> (Chairman of the U.S. Banking
> and Currency Commission for 22 years)

Permit me to issue and control the money of a nation, and I care not who makes its laws . . .
> Mayer Anselm Rothschild

I believe that banking institutions are more dangerous to our liberties than standing armies. . . .
> Thomas Jefferson, President

Whoever controls the volume of money in any country is absolute master of all industry and commerce.
> James A. Garfield, President

The price we have to pay for money is paid in liberty. ”
> Robert Louis Stevenson

The Money That Talks

It has been estimated that the personal assets of David Rockefeller are in excess of $300 million and that he oversees the family wealth of some $4 billion . . . he commands a network in 77 countries controlling assets worth more than $70 billion. With money comes power.

In 1980, Chrysler Corporation and The First Pennsylvania Bank were both rescued from bankruptcy by an infusion of Billions of dollars supplied by the U.S. Government. Ahead lies a money crash!

Straddled By Interest Payments

While in the same year, 1975, New York City lurched to the brink of bankruptcy unable to meet its almost $12 billion budget. Straddled by high interest costs, New York City has to pay almost $2 billion a year (or 17% of its budget) just for interest! New York City found itself at the mercy of the United States Government and under its precarious control.

The Diminishing Dollar

And the United States Government was not setting a good example. If the dollar was worth 100 cents in 1970 . . . by 1982 the purchasing power will only be 40 cents. A $75,000 house of today will cost over $150,000 in 1984.

The Rising World Currency

In the world market a new form of buying power is replacing the U.S. dollar. It is called SDR — Special Drawing Right. This artificial money standard is based on the values of 16 of the world's leading currencies. SDR's are not pieces of paper but rather computer transactions that control world economy!

CHANGES IN SPIRITUAL STANDARDS

11:56

66 We are just beginning to discover the virtually limitless capacities of the mind, including mystical experiences. 99

JH
Marriage Counselor
in Sex and Career

**Mind Control
Now a
Big Business**

While some may not consider it a religion, mind control programs are being hawked by more than a dozen organizations. Some are given wide publicity by TV personalities. Among them are:

Arica / Founded in 1971 by a Bolivian guru Oscar Ichaza. Arica (which means "open door") is a blend of Eastern and Western disciplines. 40-day intensive programs are offered combining physical and mental exercises and chanting mantras.

Silva Mind Control / Developed by José Silva in the 1940's; a packaged program of four 12-hour classes that relies on meditation and self-hypnosis.

**Preparing
the Mind
for Antichrist**

Est / Founded by Jack Rosenberg (who has changed his name to Werner Erhard). Most of the exercises ("processes") in *est* are aimed at dislodging trainees from their belief system. This is done by temporarily restricting food and drink; by inducing physical exhaustion and mental strain. In the *est* system, every system of meaning imposed by outside sources such as parents, school and church, is shown as an illusion. Many people believe *est's* program develops a spiritual Fascism that produces mechanical zombies who have no desires nor intentions of their own. Yet, by the end of 1976 some 85,000 *est* graduates had each spent 60 hours (and $250), experiencing this programming. In 1976 *est* grossed almost $10 million.

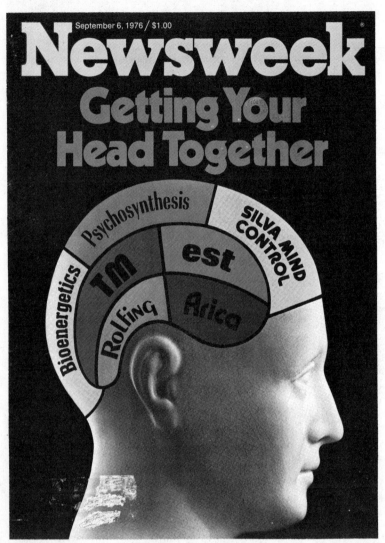

September 6, 1976 / $1.00

Newsweek

Getting Your Head Together

Psychosynthesis

Bioenergetics

TM

Rolfing

est

Arica

SILVA MIND CONTROL

More and more people are becoming involved in mind control. This trend can have very serious repercussions.

CHARTS ON REVELATION

Armageddon

Millennium

Final
Rebellion

New Heavens
and New Earth

$1

Special Report No. 8

Israel Surrounded by Hostile Nations

One look at this map clearly indicates the vulnerability of Israel to a massive attack either by Arab nations or the Soviet Union. In her desire to capture Israel's vast mineral wealth . . . one day Russia (with her allies) will invade Israel. This invasion could take place at any time now. Russia, in area, is the largest country in the world. When Russia begins her attack, God will intervene. Through an earthquake in Israel plus rain and hail, the Russian Army will be wiped out. It will take the Israelites 7 years to collect the debris. It will also take them 7 months to bury the enemy dead! See Ezekiel 38:1—39:16.

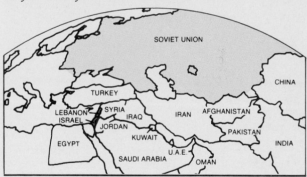

SPECIAL KIRBAN REPORT

Published by SALEM KIRBAN, Inc., Kent Road, Huntingdon Valley, Pa. 19006, U.S.A. Copyright © 1980 by Salem Kirban. Printed in U.S.A.

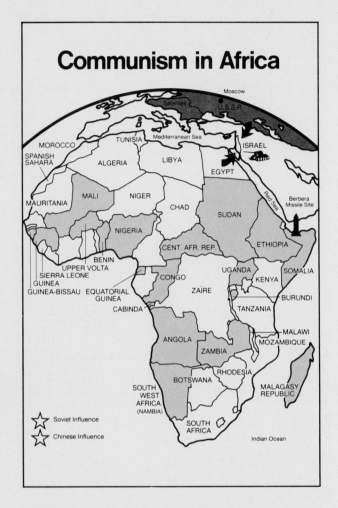

Communism in Africa

The Dangerous Dilemma in the Middle East . . .

One thing in common that the oil-rich countries of Iran, Saudi Arabia and Oman have is that they **(A)** Detest U.S. interference in their countries and **(B)** Have a strong dislike for the Soviets.

The instability of Iran and the bold Soviet invasion of Afghanistan point to the vulnerability of the world's richest pool of oil! The U.S. is banking on a *"rapid deployment"* of 110,000 men from the U.S. should an emergency occur. But no large movement of American soldiers can move 7000 miles (from the U.S.) before the Soviets move 500 miles! The Soviets, in a brief time, threw 85,000 men in Afghanistan alone!

Look at the map below. You can see that the Soviets domi-
nate the Indian Ocean and can effectively put a stranglehold
on the world's main oil sources. The 3 Arab countries (Saudi
Arabia, Iran and Oman) indirectly are aiding the Soviets in their
drive for Middle East control by refusing U.S. direct intervention
with established bases.

What's the outlook? Soviet take-over of Iraq and Syria, Iran
and Pakistan! War is not a possibility. <u>WAR IS A CERTAINTY!</u>
There is no way out. We have allowed the Russians to go too far!

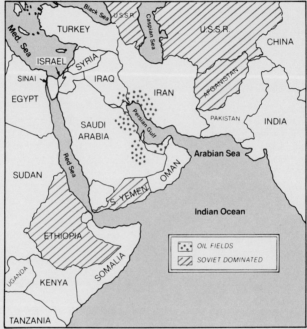

U.S.A. Copyright © 1980 by Salem Kirban.

Questions Frequently Asked Me About HEAVEN

Do Scriptures tell us how long the Marriage Supper will last?

Just as the official joining of a man to a woman is celebrated by a Marriage Supper, a banquet of rejoicing, so the union of Christ to the Church will have—reveal the scriptures—its banquet of rejoicing. Suggestions as to its length have varied from those who feel that it is a single festive meal at the start of the Millennium to those who liken it to a 1000 years of rejoicing with Christ during the entire Millennial Age. Some say it will be entirely in heaven, while the last half of the Tribulation is going on in the earth; but others have it as an affair on the earth.

The exact answer seems not to be revealed in Scripture in its details. Thus the hazzarding of opinions on such details becomes theoretical deduction at best. Such suggestions must be examined cautiously (not ridiculed—but examined). Suffice it to say that scripture is crystal clear in revealing that there will be a grand and glorious supper celebrating Christ and the Church's forever being bodily together, all the redeemed will be there, it will be sometime after the Rapture (when at last Christ takes His Church to Himself), and it will coincide with the joyous inauguration of the promised Kingdom of God.

Will we be reunited with our loved ones in Heaven? Will we live again with our mates?

Scripture indicates that there will be no more separation in Heaven! All the saints of the ages will be there. No more will friends and loved ones have to part again. No more will families have to have tearful farewells (Revelation 21:4). What a grand reunion saints in Christ will enjoy forever and forever (1 Thessalonians 4:15)!

In 1 Corinthians 15:44 we are told that in Heaven our bodies will be entirely different in nature. In Luke 20:35-36 the Lord tells us that the marriage relationship as we know it today has no place there, for there is no longer any need for the bearing of new children—death is no more and countless thousands and millions will be there who have been redeemed by Christ.

In 2 Corinthians 5:16, a key verse, we are told, "Henceforth know we no man after the flesh: yea, though we have known Christ after the flesh, yet now henceforth know we him no more." This is saying that consequently, from now on we estimate and regard no one from a purely human point of view . . . even though we once estimated Christ from a human viewpoint. We shall know one another in Heaven and be able to rejoice together in the memories of God's grace to us.

The husband will recognize his wife and the wife her husband, and it will be a loving recognition . . . they will doubtless love one another as well as others in at last a perfect love. All will be absorbed in the spiritual delights of their new condition in Christ.

There will be no need to carry photographs of loved ones in order to renew memories . . . for those Christians who have been absent for years will now be present in Heaven.

Thus, we will recognize our loved ones in Heaven but there is no Scripture which indicates we will live together as husband and wife precisely as we did on earth. Since Revelation 21:4 assures us of perfect bliss in the future world let no child of God be fearful. God made heaven for us, He loves us, He knows our needs—it will not disappoint us. It will be wonderful, and there we shall at last be with Christ unseparated forever.

Are there Scriptures that show that a believer goes to be with the Lord immediately after death?

Yes. A number of Scriptures teach this.

You recall the Lord's words of assurance to the thief who turned to Him in faith on the cross:

Verily I say unto thee, Today shalt thou be with me in paradise (Luke 23:43).

Read also our Lord's account of the rich man and Lazarus (Luke 16:22).

Another evidence is found in 2 Corinthians 5:6-8:

Therefore we are always confident, knowing that, whilst we are at home in the body, we are absent from the Lord . . . we are . . . willing rather to be absent from the body, and to be present with the Lord.

These Scriptures indicate clearly that when a believer dies, he or she goes at once to be with the Lord. Absence from the body means presence with the Lord, how wonderful! This scripture alone refutes the false doctrine of soul sleep. For, if the dead in Christ remain unconscious in some long sleep of the soul until the resurrection, then Paul could *never* have said that he was "willing rather to be absent from the body," that is, dead. Then it would be better for him to live as long as possible before the slumber of death. No, the moment a believer dies he or she is with their Lord. That is the Biblical teaching.

Bible History and Prophecy Through The Ages

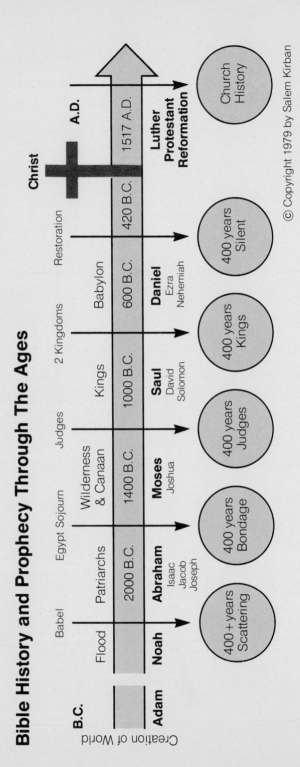

© Copyright 1979 by Salem Kirban

6

The Seven Dispensations

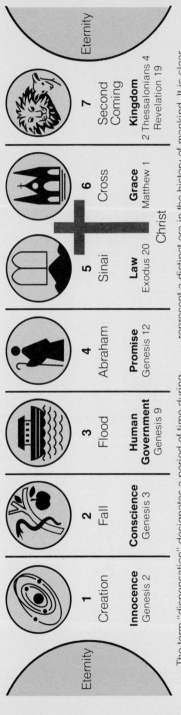

Eternity	1 Creation	2 Fall	3 Flood	4 Abraham	5 Sinai	6 Cross	7 Second Coming	Eternity
	Innocence Genesis 2	**Conscience** Genesis 3	**Human Government** Genesis 9	**Promise** Genesis 12	**Law** Exodus 20	**Grace** Matthew 1	**Kingdom** 2 Thessalonians 4 Revelation 19	

Christ

The term "dispensation" designates a period of time during which (1) God's progressive revelation to man, (2) His sovereign will made known in history, and (3) man's response to God's revelation (combined in a composite picture) represent a distinct era in the history of mankind. It is clear, however, that salvation has been by grace in every one of the dispensations.

© Copyright 1979 by Salem Kirban

7

Israel's Past, Present and Future

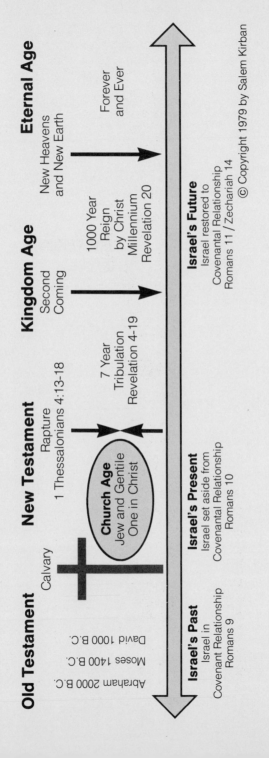

Old Testament

Abraham 2000 B.C.
Moses 1400 B.C.
David 1000 B.C.

Calvary

New Testament

Rapture
1 Thessalonians 4:13-18

7 Year
Tribulation
Revelation 4-19

Church Age
Jew and Gentile
One in Christ

Kingdom Age

Second
Coming

1000 Year
Reign
by Christ
Millennium
Revelation 20

Eternal Age

New Heavens
and New Earth

Forever
and Ever

Israel's Past
Israel in
Covenantal Relationship
Romans 9

Israel's Present
Israel set aside from
Covenantal Relationship
Romans 10

Israel's Future
Israel restored to
Covenantal Relationship
Romans 11 / Zechariah 14

© Copyright 1979 by Salem Kirban

8

Israel-Dispersed and Regathered

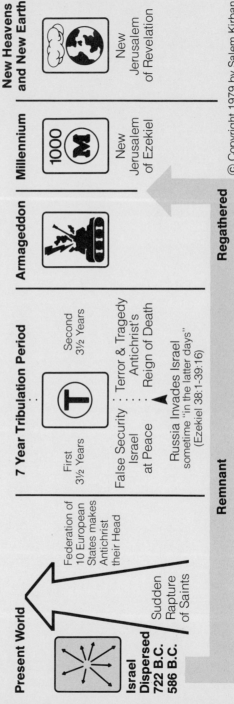

Present World

Israel Dispersed 722 B.C. 586 B.C.

Sudden Rapture of Saints

Federation of 10 European States makes Antichrist their Head

7 Year Tribulation Period

First 3½ Years

Second 3½ Years

False Security : Terror & Tragedy
Israel : Antichrist's
at Peace : Reign of Death

Russia Invades Israel sometime "in the latter days" (Ezekiel 38:1-39:16)

Armageddon

Millennium

1000

New Jerusalem of Ezekiel

New Heavens and New Earth

New Jerusalem of Revelation

Remnant

Regathered

© Copyright 1979 by Salem Kirban

9

Olivet Discourse ... An Overview

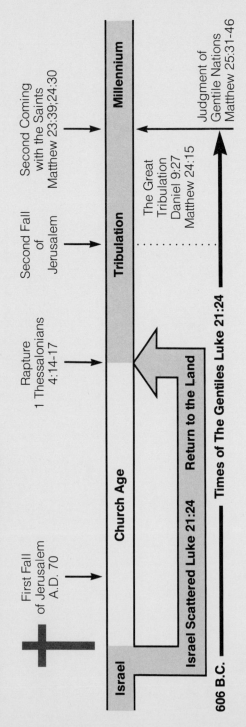

First Fall
of Jerusalem
A.D. 70

Rapture
1 Thessalonians
4:14-17

Second Fall
of
Jerusalem

Second Coming
with the Saints
Matthew 23:39;24:30

Israel | **Church Age** | **Tribulation** | **Millennium**

Israel Scattered Luke 21:24   Return to the Land

The Great
Tribulation
Daniel 9:27
Matthew 24:15

Judgment of
Gentile Nations
Matthew 25:31-46

606 B.C. ——— Times of The Gentiles Luke 21:24

Sequence of Coming Judgments

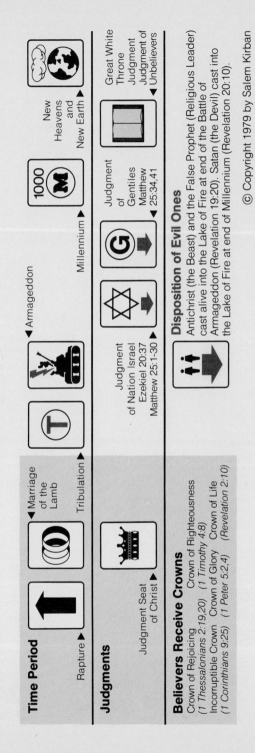

Time Period

Rapture ▲

▼ Marriage of the Lamb

Tribulation ▲

▼ Armageddon

Millennium ▲

New Heavens and New Earth ▲

▼ Great White Throne Judgment Judgment of Unbelievers

1000 (M)

Judgments

Judgment Seat of Christ ▲

Judgment of Nation Israel Ezekiel 20:37 Matthew 25:1-30 ▲

Judgment of Gentiles Matthew 25:34,41 ▲

Believers Receive Crowns

Crown of Rejoicing   Crown of Righteousness
(1 Thessalonians 2:19,20) (1 Timothy 4:8)
Incorruptible Crown Crown of Glory   Crown of Life
(1 Corinthians 9:25) (1 Peter 5:2,4)   (Revelation 2:10)

Disposition of Evil Ones

Antichrist (the Beast) and the False Prophet (Religious Leader) cast alive into the Lake of Fire at end of the Battle of Armageddon (Revelation 19:20). Satan (the Devil) cast into the Lake of Fire at end of Millennium (Revelation 20:10).

© Copyright 1979 by Salem Kirban

11

3 DECISIVE WARS

War	Participants	Occurs	Reason for War	Outcome	Scripture References
1	Russia and Allies (Arab nations, Iran, Germany) vs. Israel	Before or during first 3½ years of Tribulation Period (This could happen at any time!)	Possibly because Russia desires Israel's vast mineral wealth.	God will intervene and through an earthquake in Israel plus rain and hail, the Russian army will be wiped out. It will take the Israelites 7 years to collect the debris. It will also take them 7 months to bury the dead!	Ezekiel 38:1-39:16
2	**Armies from All Nations vs. God** at Jerusalem. **Battle of Armageddon**	At End of 7 year Tribulation Period	Flushed with power Antichrist will defy God, seek to destroy the 144,000 witnessing Jews and Jerusalem.	The Lord Jesus Christ comes down from heaven and wipes out the combined armies of more than 200 million men. The blood bath covers over 185 miles of Israel and is "even unto the horse bridles." **(Revelation 14:20)** Antichrist and the False Prophet are cast alive into the Lake of Fire. **(Revelation 19:20)** Satan is bound in the bottomless pit for 1000 years. **(Revelation 20:1-3)**	Joel 3:9, 12 Zechariah 14:1-4 Revelation 16:13-16 Revelation 19:11-21 Ezekiel 39:17-29
3	Satan vs. God. **The FINAL REBELLION**	At End of 1000 year Millennium Period	God allows Satan one more opportunity on earth to preach his deceiving message.	Satan will be successful in deceiving vast multitudes (out of those born during the millennial period) to turn away from Christ. This horde of perhaps millions of people will completely circle the Believers in Jerusalem in a state of siege. When this occurs, God brings FIRE down from Heaven killing the millions in Satan's Army. Satan is then cast into the Lake of Fire, where the False Prophet and Antichrist are, and they will be tormented day and night for ever and ever.	Revelation 20:7-10

THE JUDGMENTS OF THE TRIBULATION PERIOD

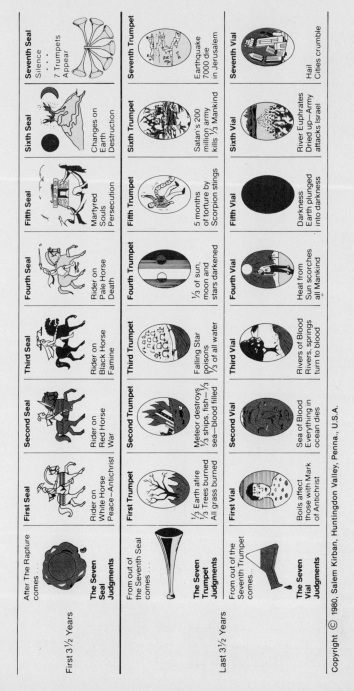

First 3½ Years

The Seven Seal Judgments — After The Rapture comes . . .

	First Seal	Second Seal	Third Seal	Fourth Seal	Fifth Seal	Sixth Seal	Seventh Seal
	Rider on White Horse Peace—Antichrist	Rider on Red Horse War	Rider on Black Horse Famine	Rider on Pale Horse Death	Martyred Souls Persecution	Changes on Earth Destruction	Silence . . . 7 Trumpets Appear

The Seven Trumpet Judgments — From out of the Seventh Seal comes . . .

	First Trumpet	Second Trumpet	Third Trumpet	Fourth Trumpet	Fifth Trumpet	Sixth Trumpet	Seventh Trumpet
	⅓ Earth afire ⅓ Trees burned All grass burned	Meteor destroys ⅓ ships, fish—⅓ sea—blood filled	Falling Star poisons ⅓ of all water	⅓ of sun, moon and stars darkened	5 months of torture by Scorpion stings	Satan's 200 million army kills ⅓ Mankind	Earthquake 7000 die in Jerusalem

Last 3½ Years

The Seven Vial Judgments — From out of the Seventh Trumpet comes . . .

	First Vial	Second Vial	Third Vial	Fourth Vial	Fifth Vial	Sixth Vial	Seventh Vial
	Boils affect those with Mark of Antichrist	Sea of Blood Everything in ocean dies	Rivers of Blood Rivers, springs turn to blood	Heat from Sun scorches all Mankind	Darkness Earth plunged into darkness	River Euphrates Dried up—Army attacks Israel	Hail Cities crumble

Copyright © 1980, Salem Kirban, Huntingdon Valley, Penna., U.S.A.

Seventieth Week of Daniel

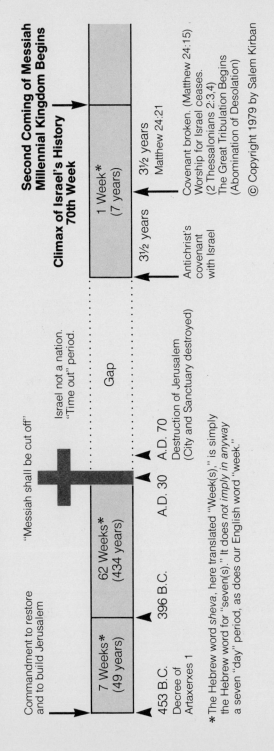

Commandment to restore and to build Jerusalem

"Messiah shall be cut off"

Israel not a nation. "Time out" period.

Second Coming of Messiah
Millennial Kingdom Begins

Climax of Israel's History
70th Week

| 7 Weeks* (49 years) | 62 Weeks* (434 years) | | Gap | 1 Week* (7 years) | |

453 B.C.
Decree of Artaxerxes 1

396 B.C.

A.D. 30

A.D. 70
Destruction of Jerusalem
(City and Sanctuary destroyed)

3½ years

3½ years
Matthew 24:21

Antichrist's covenant with Israel

Covenant broken. (Matthew 24:15)
Worship for Israel ceases.
(2 Thessalonians 2:3,4)
The Great Tribulation Begins
(Abomination of Desolation)

© Copyright 1979 by Salem Kirban

*The Hebrew word *sheva*, here translated "Week(s)," is simply the Hebrew word for "seven(s)." It does *not imply in anyway* a seven "day" period, as does our English word "week."

14

<table>
<tr><td>

CHRIST

</td><td>

ANTICHRIST

</td></tr>
<tr><td>

Christ came from **Above**.
John 6:38.

</td><td>

Antichrist ascends from **The Pit**.
Revelation 11:7.

</td></tr>
<tr><td>

Christ came in His **Father's** name.
John 5:43.

</td><td>

Antichrist comes in his **Own** name.
John 5:43.

</td></tr>
<tr><td>

Christ **Humbled** Himself.
Philippians 2:8.

</td><td>

Antichrist **Exalts** himself.
2 Thessalonians 2:4.

</td></tr>
<tr><td>

Christ **Despised**.
Isaiah 53:3; Luke 23:18

</td><td>

Antichrist **Admired**.
Revelation 13:3, 4.

</td></tr>
<tr><td>

Christ **Exalted**.
Philippians 2:9.

</td><td>

Antichrist **Cast Down to Hell**.
Isaiah 14:14, 15; Rev. 19:20.

</td></tr>
<tr><td>

Christ to do His **Father's** will.
John 6:38.

</td><td>

Antichrist to do His **Own** will.
Daniel 11:36.

</td></tr>
<tr><td>

Christ came to **Save**.
Luke 19:10.

</td><td>

Antichrist comes to **Destroy**.
Daniel 8:24.

</td></tr>
<tr><td>

Christ is the **Good Shepherd**.
John 10:4-15.

</td><td>

Antichrist, the **Idol** (evil) Shepherd.
Zechariah 11:16,17.

</td></tr>
<tr><td>

Christ is the **"True Vine."**
John 15:1.

</td><td>

Antichrist, the **"Vine of the Earth."** Revelation 14:18.

</td></tr>
<tr><td>

Christ is the **"Truth."**
John 14:6.

</td><td>

Antichrist is the **"Lie."**
2 Thessalonians 2:11

</td></tr>
<tr><td>

Christ, the **"Holy One."**
Mark 1:24

</td><td>

Antichrist is the **"Lawless One."**
2 Thessalonians 2:8, A.S.V.

</td></tr>
<tr><td>

Christ is the **"Man of Sorrows."** Isaiah 53:3.

</td><td>

Antichrist is the **"Man of Sin."**
2 Thessalonians 2:3.

</td></tr>
<tr><td>

Christ is the **"Son of God."**
Luke 1:35.

</td><td>

Antichrist is the **"Son of Perdition."**
2 Thessalonians 2:3.

</td></tr>
<tr><td>

Christ, **"The Mystery of Godliness,"** is **God** manifest in the flesh.
1 Timothy 3:16.

</td><td>

Antichrist, **"The Mystery of Iniquity,"** will be **Satan** manifest in the flesh.
2 Thessalonians 2:7.

</td></tr>
</table>

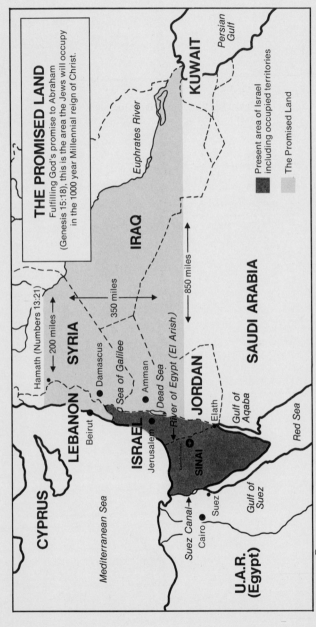

THE PROMISED LAND

Fulfilling God's promise to Abraham (Genesis 15:18), this is the area the Jews will occupy in the 1000 year Millennial reign of Christ.

Present area of Israel including occupied territories

The Promised Land

CYPRUS

LEBANON

Beirut

Mediterranean Sea

ISRAEL

Jerusalem

SINAI

Suez Canal

Cairo

Suez

Gulf of Suez

U.A.R. (Egypt)

Red Sea

Hamath (Numbers 13:21)

← 200 miles →

SYRIA

Damascus

Sea of Galilee

Amman

Dead Sea

River of Egypt (El Arish)

JORDAN

Elath

Gulf of Aqaba

← 350 miles →

Euphrates River

IRAQ

850 miles

SAUDI ARABIA

KUWAIT

Persian Gulf

Copyright © 1980, Salem Kirban, Huntingdon Valley, Penna., U.S.A.

16

NOW! AT LAST! A BIBLE WITH 2000 PAGES OF HELPS TO MEET EVERY NEED IN YOUR LIFE!

Salem Kirban's
REFERENCE BIBLE
KING JAMES VERSION

Now, the world's best **seller** will become the best **read** in your home! Salem Kirban has taken the beloved King James Version and added 2000 pages of crystal-clear Commentary. Here are 10 reasons why many acclaim that this Bible is the first really new Bible since the 1909 Scofield. Over 500 photos and charts **Full Color.** Only 1¾″ thick. Handy to carry to church!

10 EXCLUSIVE Features NO OTHER BIBLE HAS!

1. Commentary on Every Page Unlocks Guidelines for Living

Salem Kirban
In his clear, descriptive style, Salem Kirban's Commentary Notes appear on **over** 1000 of the Bible text pages. He is the author of over 35 books!

Gary G. Cohen
Dr. Cohen clearly explains the 100 most difficult Bible passages. Dr. Cohen is Executive Vice President of Clearwater Christian College.

Charles Haddon Spurgeon
The most famous preacher of the 19th century. His devotional Commentary *(written during his greatest trials)* are on over 300 pages.

2. Promise Verses In Margin

When you need faith and courage . . . often the Promise Verses in the Bible are hard to find because these gems lie buried in the text. We have highlighted these Promise Verses in yellow (in the text) and **also** repeated the same verse in the MARGIN of the same page. Now, by leafing through your Bible, you can each day

 Scattering of Israel

 NOW Current World

 Continual Promise

 Rapture

 Armageddon

 Judgment Seat of Christ

 Marriage of the Lamb

Judgment of Nation Israel

Sample Page — Actual Page Size: 6″ x 9″

select a Promise To Live By! See sample page in this column.

3. Time Period Symbols

The Bible is confusing to many because they do not realize that the text refers to 3 basic Time Periods (past, present and future). Within these 3 Time Periods are at least 15 **further** Time Divisions! In the margin of each page of The Salem Kirban REFERENCE BIBLE, the Time Symbol Picture helps you identify the correct Time Period . . . making God's promises so much richer to you and to your loved ones.

4. Rare, Old Bible Etchings

Unusual etchings of Bible scenes designed by craftsmen over 100 years ago. Enjoy the same etchings your great grandparents found joy and comfort in!

5. Full Color Holy Land Photographs

Vivid photographs taken by Salem Kirban reveal the beauty of the Promised Land as it is **right now** . . . today!

6. Full Color Charts on Future Events

Over 50 Charts including the 21 Tribulation Judgments, Three Coming Decisive Wars, The Three Heavens, The Resurrections. A few are picture below in reduced size.

Time Period Views of The Prophets
The prophets had a twofold ministry. They exposed the sins of their own time. They also revealed the future (as God revealed it to them).

When reading the Books written by the 16 prophets (Isaiah through Malachi) this Chart will help you understand the scope of time periods referred to by the prophet.

© Copyright 1979 by Salem Kirban

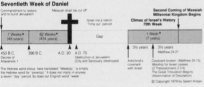

Seventieth Week of Daniel

© Copyright 1979 by Salem Kirban

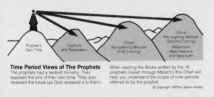

Bible History and Prophecy Through The Ages

© Copyright 1979 by Salem Kirban

380 Page Commentary on The Book of REVELATION

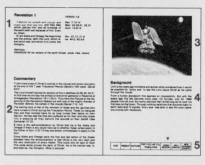

The last book in the Bible, **Revelation,** deals with future events and is the most difficult book for many to understand. We have Visualized the book by **1** placing only 2 verses on each page **2** writing a clear Commentary **3** including an explanatory illustration **4** tying the verses in to current events and **5** by a red arrow, pointing to the proper Time Period!

8. Major Doctrines Explained

There are at least 28 major Doctrines in the Bible. These DOCTRINES are explained in Commentary units marked with this Symbol placed next to identifying verse!

9. Major Attributes Explained

There are 17 Attributes (or characteristics) that identify God! Each ATTRIBUTE is explained in Commentary units marked with this Symbol placed next to identifying verse!

10. Extra NEW TESTAMENT Commentary

As an added bonus, you will discover **100 added pages** of special New Testament Commentary. All in FULL COLOR. Includes many Charts, Maps and Graphs!

The Image of Daniel 2

606 ± B.C.
Gold — Nebuchadnezzar's
Babylon (Unquestioned
obedience to one absolute
sovereign)

536 ± B.C.
Silver — The dual Empire of
the Medes & Persians
(The 2 arms!)

336 B.C.
Copper — The Greek
Empire

200 ± B.C.
Iron Legs United —
Roman Republic & Empire

300 ± A.D.
Iron Legs Divided —
Western & Eastern
Roman Empire

476 & 1453 A.D. (They fall)

Iron Legs Cracking —
European States

Iron & Clay Feet — End-time
Lawlessness (Communism)?

10 Toes — Revived Rome
Confederacy

A.D.?

THE STAGES OF EARTH

THIS PRESENT EARTH

ETERNITY

ORIGINAL EARTH

"In the beginning God created the heaven and the earth."
(Genesis 1:1)

EARTH CURSED MAN SINS

Genesis 3

ANTEDELUVIAN
Before the Flood **AGE**
WICKEDNESS INCREASES

"And (God) spared not the old world, but saved Noah the eighth person, a preacher of righteousness, bringing in the flood upon the world of the ungodly."
(II Peter 2:5)

FLOOD JUDGMENT

". . . I will cause it to rain upon the earth . . . and every living substance that I have made will I destroy from off the face of the earth."
(Genesis 7:4)

PRESENT EVIL AGE

"(Christ) Who gave Himself for our sins, that He might deliver us from this present evil world . . ."
(Galatians 1:4)

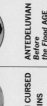

TRIBULATION PERIOD JUDGMENT

"Then shall the Lord go forth, and fight against those nations . . . and His feet shall stand . . . upon the Mount of Olives . . ."
(Zechariah 14:3,4)

1000 YEAR MILLENNIAL AGE

". . . and they lived and reigned with Christ a thousand years."
(Revelation 20:4)

EARTH DESTROYED BY FIRE

". . . the elements shall melt with fervent heat, the earth also and the works that are therein shall be burned up."
(II Peter 3:10)

ETERNITY

THE NEW HEAVENS AND NEW EARTH

"And I saw a new heaven and a new earth: for the first heaven and the first earth were passed away; and there was no more sea."
(Revelation 21:1)

THREE VIEWS ON THE RAPTURE*

These are NOT millennial positions but merely three of the views on the exact time of Christ's return within the PRE-MILLENNIAL camp. Correctness on these positions have nothing to do with the salvation of a sinner.

THE RAPTURE POSITIONS	WHAT DOES IT MEAN	WHAT EACH GROUP BELIEVES	WHY MANY BELIEVERS HOLD TO THE PRE-TRIBULATION RAPTURE VIEW
POST TRIBULATION RAPTURE	The Church (believers) will be raptured AFTER the 7 year Tribulation Period.	The Church will go through the awful Tribulation. (Matthew 24:21).	The Church is to be spared God's wrath (Romans 9:5). Since the entire 7 year Tribulation Period is a pouring out of God's wrath (Revelation 6:17), the Rapture must remove the Church before this pouring occurs. Genesis 19:22 shows this principle. The angel could not begin to destroy Sodom until Lot was safely removed from the area!
MID TRIBULATION RAPTURE	The Church (believers) will be raptured in the midst of the 7 year Tribulation Period.	The Church will be saved only from the last 3½ year "Great Tribulation." (Matthew 24:21).	
PRE TRIBULATION RAPTURE	The Church (believers) will be raptured before the 7 year Tribulation Period starts.	The Church will be saved from the entire 7 year Tribulation. (Matthew 24:21).	

On the time of the RAPTURE, which is a complex topic, interested readers should refer to:
KEPT FROM THE HOUR, Gerald B. Stanton (Toronto: Evangelical Publishers, 1964);
THINGS TO COME. J. Dwight Pentecost (Grand Rapids, Michigan: Zondervan Publishing Company, 1958);
THE RAPTURE QUESTION, John F. Walvoord (Grand Rapids, Michigan: Zondervan Publishing Company, 1957);
UNDERSTANDING REVELATION, Gary G. Cohen, Executive Vice-President, Clearwater Christian College, Clearwater, Florida 33515).

*RAPTURE: This refers to the time when believing Christians (both dead and alive) will "In the twinkling of an eye" rise up to meet Christ in the air (I Thessalonians 4:13-18).

Chart by Dr. Gary G. Cohen

THREE VIEWS ON THE MILLENNIUM

THE MILLENNIUM POSITIONS	WHAT DOES IT MEAN	WHAT EACH GROUP BELIEVES	OBJECTION OR SUPPORT
POST MILLENNIALISM	Christ will come to establish His Kingdom on Earth AFTER (Post) the 1000 Years (Millennium).	The earth will get better and better through the spread of the Gospel, and Christ will come to claim His Kingdom after 1000 years of peace has transpired.	Naïve. The earth is not getting better; and the Bible does not teach that it is (II Timothy 3:1-7).
A MILLENNIALISM	There will be NO FUTURE Earthly 1000 year Reign (Millennium). (In Greek "A" at the beginning of a word means "NO.")	The Millennium is *NOW!* Peace on earth exists in the Church; and Satan is NOW bound so that he cannot prevent the spread of the Gospel.	Revelation 20:3 says that Satan goes to prison "that he should deceive the nations no more." Look at Cuba, China and Russia. Satan is not NOW in prison.
PRE MILLENNIALISM	Christ will come personally to judge the wicked and to establish His Kingdom BEFORE (Pre) the 1000 years (Millennium) begins.	The earth is getting worse, and the Kingdom age cannot begin until Christ comes to destroy the wicked.	This is the teaching of the Bible. Christ will come (Revelation 19: 11-21) and then the Kingdom will be set up (Revelation 20).

THESE POSITIONS HAVE *NOTHING* TO DO WITH THE SALVATION OF A SINNER.

JUDGMENT DAYS

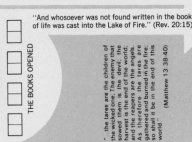

JUDGMENT OF UNBELIEVERS

BOOK OF LIFE

THE BOOKS OPENED

"And whosoever was not found written in the book of life was cast into the Lake of Fire." (Rev. 20:15)

LAKE OF FIRE

". . . the tares are the children of the wicked one; The enemy that sowed them is the devil; the harvest is the end of the world; and the reapers are the angels. As therefore the tares are gathered and burned in the fire; so shall it be in the end of this world" (Matthew 13:38-40)

1000 YEAR MILLENNIUM

REWARD JUDGMENTS FOR BELIEVERS

"and I will dwell in the house of the Lord for ever" (Psalm 23:6)

INCORRUPTIBLE CROWN (Victor's Crown)
". . . every man that striveth for the mastery is temperate in all things . . . they do it to obtain a corruptible crown; we an INCORRUPTIBLE." (I Corinthians 9:25)

CROWN OF REJOICING (Soul Winner's Crown)
". . . what is our hope . . . or crown of rejoicing? Are not even ye in the presence of our Lord Jesus Christ at His coming? For ye are our glory and joy." (I Thessalonians 2:19, 20)

CROWN OF RIGHTEOUSNESS
"Henceforth there is laid up for me a crown of righteousness, which the Lord, the righteous judge, shall give me at that day: and not to me only, but unto all them also that love His appearing." (II Timothy 4:8)

CROWN OF GLORY (Crown for Service)
"Feed the flock of God which is among you . . . (be) examples to the flock . . . And when the chief Shepherd shall appear, ye shall receive a crown of glory that fadeth not away." (I Peter 5:2-4)

CROWN OF LIFE (Martyr's Crown)
". . . the devil shall cast some of you into prison, that ye may be tried . . . be thou faithful unto death, and I will give thee a crown of life." (Revelation 2:10)

"Every man's work shall be made manifest . . . because it shall be revealed by fire . . . if any man's work abide . . . he shall receive a reward . . . if any man's work shall be burned, he shall suffer loss: but he himself shall be saved; yet so as by fire." (I Corinthians 3:13-15)

GOLD | PRECIOUS STONES
SILVER

WOOD | HAY | STUBBLE

RAPTURE
BELIEVERS meet CHRIST in the air

THE RESURRECTIONS

Heaven

Paradise

Believers who have died before the Rapture. Present in a celestial, spiritual body.*

▲ "And Jesus said unto him, Verily I say unto thee, To-day shalt thou be with me in paradise."
Luke 23:43

"We are confident, I say, and willing rather to be absent from the body, and to be present with the Lord."
2 Corinthians 5:8

Rapture

Believers meet with Christ in the air
1 Thessalonians 4:16

"...the dead in Christ shall rise First..."

"Then we which are alive and remain shall be caught up together with them in the clouds to meet the Lord in the air....." 1 Thessalonians 4:16-17

Judgment Seat of Christ

"For we must all appear before the judgment seat of Christ...."
2 Corinthians 5:10
Believers now in New Bodies

Resurrection of Tribulation Saints
Daniel 12:1-2

Marriage of the Lamb
Revelation 19:7-9

Christ Returns to Earth with His Saints
1 Thessalonians 3:13; Zechariah 14:4

Great White Throne

"And whosoever was not found written in the Book of Life was cast into the Lake of Fire."
Revelation 20:15

Unbelievers cast into Lake of Fire eternally

Resurrection of the Dead Unbelievers
Revelation 20:11-13; Jude 6

▲ "And I saw the dead, small and great, stand before God; and the books were opened; and another book was opened, which is the book of life: and the dead were judged out of those things which were written in the books, according to their works.
And the sea gave up the dead which were in it; and death and hell delivered up the dead which were in them: and they were judged every man according to their works."
Revelation 20:12-13

Resurrection and Ascension of Christ into Heaven
Acts 1:1-11
Matthew 27:50-53

*Physical body remains in grave awaiting Rapture

(Matthew 27:52-53 tells of others who were resurrected after Christ— these were the wave-sheaf of the harvest to come. Leviticus 23:10-11.)

| About A.D. 30 | This Present Age | A.D.? | Rapture | Seven Year Tribulation Period | Mount of Olives Armageddon | 1000 Year Millennial Age | With Satan Antichrist and False Prophet |

Copyright © 1973, Salem Kirban

25

THREE HEAVENS

The word *heaven* is used hundreds of times in the Bible. The primary meaning of *heaven* is "*that which is above.*" In God's Word *heaven* refers to one of three major realms as noted below.

THE HEAVENS	WHERE IS IT	SOME REFERENCES IN SCRIPTURE
THE ATMOSPHERIC HEAVENS	The atmosphere which surrounds the globe. Our troposphere is a blanket of air around earth. It is no higher than 20 miles above the earth. Most clouds are within 7 miles of the earth.	The Israelites were told that the land they were to possess "is a land of hills and valleys and drinketh water of the rain from heaven" (Deut. 11:11). See also Deut. 11:17, II Chron. 7:13, Isa. 55:9-11, Psalm 147:8, Matthew 24:30, Zach. 2:6.
THE CELESTIAL HEAVENS	This is the sphere in which the sun and moon and stars appear. I Kings 8:27 speaks of the Celestial Heavens when it says, "Behold, the heaven of heavens cannot contain God."	"And God said, Let there be lights in the firmament of the heaven to divide the day from the night..." (Genesis 1:14). "... Look now toward heaven, and tell the stars, if thou be able to number them..." (Genesis 15:5). See also Hebrews 1:10, Psalm 33:6, Isaiah 14:12, Amos 5:26 and Jeremiah 23:24.
THE BELIEVERS HEAVEN (The Abode of God)	This is characterized by holiness because God dwells there. Believers also will dwell in God's heaven because they have been made holy by the grace of God. Jesus assured us of the *reality* of this place (John 14:2).	"... I dwell in the high and holy place, with him also that is of a contrite and humble spirit ..." (Isaiah 57:15). "Look down from heaven, and behold from the habitation of thy holiness and of thy glory ..." (Isaiah 63:15). See also Exodus 20:22, Deut. 4:36, Matthew 3:17, Matthew 14:19, Acts 7:55 and John 3:27.

For a fuller treatment of this subject we recommend: THE BIBLICAL DOCTRINE OF HEAVEN, Wilbur M. Smith, Published by MOODY PRESS, Chicago, Illinois

KIRBAN
REPORTS

HOW TO SECURE these Special Reports: There are 14 Special Reports described on these pages. All are written by Salem Kirban. Reports are $1 each. **Minimum Order accepted is $10.** Save by buying in quantity; 25 copies/$20; 50 copies/$37; 100 copies/$50. **You may mix titles to get maximum discount.** Check must accompany order. Order Forms are on last page of this Report.
SALEM KIRBAN, Inc.
Kent Rd., Huntingdon Valley, Pa. 19006

EXTRA BONUS Can Be Yours!
If you respond within 10 days!

Some of the chapters in **I PREDICT!**

- The Year You Change To A New Currency!
- Why Satan Wants To Control Christian Schools!
- The Day A Dictator Rules The United States!
- Why The U.S. May Not Exist In The Year 2000!
- Will 1982 Be The Year Of The MARK?
- How Your Life Will Change Drastically SOON!
- Will World War 3 Occur Before 1982?

I
PREDICT

1980's

TO RECEIVE: (1) Clip this Coupon (2) ATTACH to your Order Form when you order. I PREDICT will be sent you as an Extra Bonus! But you must respond within 10 days with $10 order or more.

EXTRA BONUS Can Be Yours!

If you respond within 10 days!

666 (New Pictorial Format)

The entire book, **666,** by Salem Kirban has now been transformed into a FULL COLOR Pictorial Format. This 64 page Quality Paperback is excellent for young and old alike. It graphically describes the Tribulation Period and how the forces of Antichrist create a holocaust of horror.

TO RECEIVE: (1) Clip this Coupon (2) AT-TACH to your Order Form. 666 will be sent as an Extra Bonus! But you must respond within 10 days with an order for $25 or more. I PREDICT will also be sent automatically.

SALEM KIRBAN'S

666

Special Report No. **1**

HUMANISM ... SINISTER, SUBTLE SEDUCTION

Humanism is a deadly philosophy . . . a philosophy that is often used by Satan to deaden the effectiveness of Christian witness. It is a real threat to the Christian School movement. Yet most believers in Christ have no idea how dangerous Humanism really is!

Humanists do not believe in God. They worship the creature rather than the Creator. They endorse abortion, genetic engineering, day care centers. They seek to break the family unit and its discipline. Distribute this Special Newsletter in your Church and School.

TO ORDER: Reports are $1 each. Minimum order accepted is $10. You may mix Reports to achieve 10 copy minimum.

SALEM KIRBAN, Kent Rd., Huntingdon Valley, Pa. 19006

Special Report No. **2**

THE TRILATERIAL COMMISSION
America's New Secret Government

The Trilateral Commission is an extension of the Council on Foreign Relations (CFR). Its ultimate goal is to incorporate Japan, Canada, the United States and the Common Market nations of Europe into a one-world socialistic governmental web.

The name, TRILATERAL, is derived from the fact that the leaders come from three democratic areas of the world . . . the United States, Western Europe and Japan. David Rockefeller hand-picked this elite group of some 250 individuals to begin this organization. They are world shapers!

TO ORDER: Reports are $1 each. Minimum order accepted is $10. You may mix Reports to achieve 10 copy minimum.

SALEM KIRBAN, Kent Rd., Huntingdon Valley, Pa. 19006

Special Report No. **3**

THE POWER SEEKERS . . . The Bilderbergers & CFR

The Bilderbergers, the CFR, the Trilateralists all have one thing in common . . . they are secret societies. The Bilderbergers have always been directed by Prince Bernhard of the Netherlands. The Bilderbergers favor an international money system called the "bancor system."

They predicted the recession and many believe both they and the CFR were influential in the control of oil and the rapid price rises of gasoline and heating oils. The CFR seeks an ultimate world order into a united nations. Antichrist will head such a European union!

TO ORDER: Reports are $1 each. Minimum order accepted is $10. You may mix Reports to achieve 10 copy minimum.

SALEM KIRBAN, Kent Rd., Huntingdon Valley, Pa. 19006

Special Report No. ④

THE ILLUMINATI

In recent years in Christian circles there have been hushed whispers about the conspiracy of the **ILLUMINATI.** Many believe their aims are to control the world through their arch leader, Satan! This Report traces the history of the **ILLUMINATI** and it may surprise you!

The Illuminati power structure has infiltrated into the United States, according to some reports. Did the Illuminati engineer both World War 1 and World War 2? And are they now planning World War 3? Is the current Middle East crisis part of this sinister plan?

TO ORDER: Reports are $1 each. Minimum order accepted is $10. You may mix Reports to achieve 10 copy minimum.

SALEM KIRBAN, Kent Rd., Huningdon Valley, Pa. 19006

Special Report No. ⑤

HOW THE MONEY MANIPULATORS KEEP YOU POOR!

We are now living in the Age of ANTICHRIST. One real indication of this is that the United States is now controlled, in large part, by powerful foreign interests.

About 200 years ago, Benjamin Franklin wrote that the conspiracy plan that would develop would be: *". . . get first all the people's money, then all their lands, and then make them and their children your servants forever!"* Reveals why the Federal Reserve is neither Federal nor Reserve! The 6-Point Plan to reduce you to POVERTY!

TO ORDER: Reports are $1 each. Minimum order accepted is $10. You may mix Reports to achieve 10 copy minimum.

SALEM KIRBAN, Kent Rd., Huntingdon Valley, Pa. 19006

Special Report No. ⑥

THE SATANIC TRINITY EXPOSED

One of these days some great leader, admired by the world as a man of peace, will settle the Arab-Israeli dispute. Watch out when this event happens. For this man will become known as the **Antichrist.** His sweet words of peace will soon lead to the most devastating seven years of terror.

Antichrist is a part of the Satanic Trinity *(just as Christ is part of the Heavenly Trinity).* The counterfeit Trinity is Satan, Antichrist and the False Prophet. A revealing study of their strategy, that has already begun!

TO ORDER: Reports are $1 each. Minimum order accepted is $10. You may mix Reports to achieve 10 copy minimum.

SALEM KIRBAN, Kent Rd., Huntingdon Valley, Pa. 19006

30

Special Report No. **10**

WHAT IS HEAVEN LIKE?

You hear very few messages preached on Heaven. And very few books are written on this subject. That is why you will find this Special Report so heartwarming.

Heaven is a place where believers will receive a new body. There will be no more death, no more tears, no more separation from loved ones in Christ, no more illness, and no night! But there will be so much more! How will your body differ from your present body? Will you recognize your loved ones? These questions and many more are answered fully!

TO ORDER: Reports are $1 each. Minimum order accepted is $10. You may mix Reports to achieve 10 copy minimum.

SALEM KIRBAN, Kent Rd., Huntingdon Valley, Pa. 19006

Special Report No. **11**

WHAT IS THE TRIBULATION LIKE?

The Tribulation Period will unleash a holocaust of horror such as the world has never seen! It will usher in Antichrist and the False Prophet. Everyone will be forced to wear an identifying Mark on their right hand or forehead or they will not be able to buy or sell!

Already we are witnessing the beginning of these sorrows. Events happening right now are preparing us for the Tribulation when every life will be controlled by Government. You owe it to yourself to know exactly what lies ahead in the not too distant future!

TO ORDER: Reports are $1 each. Minimum order accepted is $10. You may mix Reports to achieve 10 copy minimum.

SALEM KIRBAN, Kent Rd., Huntingdon Valley, Pa. 19006

Special Report No. **12**

RUSSIA'S RISE TO RUIN!

The saddest fact about Russia's rise in these Last Days is that she will destroy the independent status of the United States and force us to join the Common Market nations as an European conglomerate! Such a move will, of course, usher in the rise of Antichrist.

Now! You can follow Russia's path of conquest through this Special Report. Watch as she topples country after country with her final aim the destruction of Israel and the control of Mid-East oil fields. A revealing study. Includes charts and maps.

TO ORDER: Reports are $1 each. Minimum order accepted is $10. You may mix Reports to achieve 10 copy minimum.

SALEM KIRBAN, Kent Rd., Huntingdon Valley, Pa. 19006

Special Report No. **13**

THE SOON COMING BIRTH HATCHERIES

The day will come when an individual will not be allowed to have children as they wish. They will need a special permit from authorities. They will then be injected with a *"release drug"* that will allow conception to take place.

Soon guidelines will be drawn for birth hatcheries to produce genetically *"pure"* babies. Man will seek to improve on God and develop a Master Race. Human babies may be gestated in cows. Sperm banks will become a way of life.

TO ORDER: Reports are $1 each. Minimum order accepted is $10. You may mix Reports to achieve $10 minimum.

SALEM KIRBAN, Kent Rd., Huntingdon Valley, Pa. 19006

Special Report No. **14**

QUESTIONS ASKED ME ON PROPHECY

What is meant by *". . . this generation shall not pass till all these things be fulfilled"*? How does the United States fit into Bible prophecy? Who will be Antichrist?

Where will resurrected Believers live during the Millennium? Will we live again with our mates in Heaven? Are there Scriptures that show that a Believer goes to be with the Lord immediately after death? Do those who have already gone on to be with Christ know what is going on here on earth right now?

TO ORDER: Reports are $1 each. Minimum order accepted is $10. You may mix Reports to achieve $10 minimum.

SALEM KIRBAN, Kent Rd., Huntingdon Valley, Pa. 19006

LIST quantity you desire next to each Report Number below. *(Such as* __10__**(4)***).* Reports are $1 each. **Minimum order accepted is $10.**

RESPONSE FORM

—**(1)**   —**(2)**   —**(3)**   —**(4)**   —**(5)**   —**(6)**   —**(7)**
—**(8)**   —**(9)**   —**(10)**   —**(11)**   —**(12)**   —**(13)**   —**(14)**

☐ Enclosed is my check for $_____ (include $1 for postage).

☐ Send me 1 copy of all 14 Reports. Enclosed is $15 ($1 for postage).

Mr./Mrs./Miss _____ Please PRINT

Address _____

City _____ State _____ ZIP _____

SALEM KIRBAN, Inc.
Kent Rd., Huntingdon Valley, Pa. 19006

Save Up To 70%
BULK PRICES!

Reports	$1 each
50 copies	$ 37
100 copies	$ 50
500 copies	$200
1000 copies	$300

You may mix Titles to get maximum discount.

COUNTDOWN 11:56 TO RAPTURE

MIND CONTROL

TM . . . A Wolf in Sheep's Clothing?

There may be perhaps over 1 million people in the U.S. who practice transcendental meditation (TM). TM, brought to this country by Maharishi Mahesh Yogi, is now growing at the rate of some 30,000 new students each month. There are over 370 TM centers in the U.S. and over 6000 teachers.

The TM movement began around 1958. The Maharishi's early visitors included the Beatles, the Rolling Stones and even Joe Namath and Marlon Brando. This exposure, coupled with nationwide TV via the Merv Griffin show, accelerated its growth in the U.S.

Steering People Towards Hinduism

TM demands that its followers sit still for 20 minutes each morning and evening and silently repeat, over and over again, their specially assigned Sanskrit word, or mantra. Adherents claim this simple exercise is a cure-all for almost anything from high blood pressure to alcoholism and sexual problems.

TM is Big Business!

The Maharishi has started the Maharishi International University in Fairfield, Iowa. It occupies a 185-acre campus and has about 700 students. The American TM movements operates under the World Plan Executive Council and enjoys revenues of over $15 million annually and reaches into over 100 college campuses. In the New York Catskill Mountains, it has a 35-room hotel with a sophisticated printing plant and a sound recording complex that can compete with most TV networks. TM sessions start at $125.

11:56

66 We're here to stay and the religious community had . . . well better find that out. There's no way atheism will die now.
Madalyn Murray O'Hair

Money, money, money, making money . . . to the north, money; to the south, money; to the east, money; to the west, money. Don't wait for pie in the sky by-and-by when you die. Get your pie now — with ice cream on top! The lack of money is the root of all evil. 99
Rev. Ike
(Frederick J. Eikerenkoetter, 2nd)

Towards a Civil Religion

A recent convention of the Religious Education Association, held in Philadelphia, brought together more than 800 men and women of all faiths.

The main theme of the convention was "civil religion."

This concept is growing in many so-called religious circles. A civil religion, they argue, would transcend individual religions and could be practiced by all Americans . . . even in public schools. The one prerequisite to accepting a "civil religion," its proponents argue, is that: "both traditional and civil faiths must accept the idea that they do not possess the only truth."

They believe that they can see even those religious groups with strong dogmatic traditions begin to weaken and they believe that their civil religion aims will be achieved before the end of this century.

Growing Popularity of Cults

Meanwhile religious cults have become a magnet for many youths. Mystic sects that offer love and joy to the U.S. young are getting a big response. It is estimated that almost 5 million Americans, mostly in their late teens or early 20's, are involved in over 500 new cults.

Many of these cults have their origin in Oriental cultures while others are begun by authoritarian-type individuals who seek to impose their discipline on unwary youth who have already gone the route of drugs, sex and moral irresponsibility.

We would like to thank the 300,000 of you who came to "Meet us at the Monument"

On September 18, 1976, at the Washington Monument, Sun Myung Moon attracted some 300,000 people. Many became followers.

Moon . . . the Self-Announced Saviour of America

The place is Yankee Stadium. A chunky, Korean man harangues the crowd of almost 25,000 people for more than an hour. He speaks in Korean, an interpreter by his side. "God Bless America" banners cover the stadium. Young people cheer as if on command. His name: Sun Myung Moon.

Membership Escalating As Moonies Sacrifice

In September, 1976, in Washington, D.C., some 50,000 "Moonies," (Moon followers) came to the mass rally held at the Washington Monument. This was the climax rally of his 4-year introduction to the U.S. In 1972, when he first brought his message to America, some 30,000 youth became his followers. Now he has a worldwide membership of over 2 million. Many give up jobs and family to live in centers, bought by the church. They sleep in sleeping bags. Their life is austere. They become prime targets for mind control as they listen to 6-8 hours of lecture daily. He calls his church *The Unification Church*. Unification teaching eradicates Hell. It promises that even Lucifer will one day be reclaimed. It attacks family friends, jobs, wealth and comfort as Satan's tools to draw one away from God. It generates allegiance to Sun Myung Moon, whom they believe Jesus gave the task of completing His unfinished work.

While Moon Lives in Luxury

Moon and his 4th wife and 8 children live in a luxurious 25-room estate overlooking the Hudson River in New York. From here he manages millions of dollars. In 1975 alone, his over 30,000 U.S. member sales force turned a $10 million profit!

11:57

66 BELLY DANCING - Tues. 1:00-2:00 p.m. (Beginners) Tues. 2:00-3:00 p.m. (Advanced) Fellowship Hall. Ladies! Try an exciting escape into another culture.

BALLET (Elementary) Thurs. 7:00-8:00 p.m. Fellowship Hall. . . . Bring practice ballet slippers and appropriate attire.

YOGA I - Wed. 9:30-10:45 a.m.
YOGA II - Wed. 10:45-12 Noon
Yoga is a science that correlates mind and body.

BASIC ASTROLOGY - Thurs. 7:30-9:30 p.m. For Adults and Teenagers. Learn the history of Astrology, its correct application & intelligent approach. Learn to erect your own chart & get to know which signs of the Zodiac have the most potential for you. 99

From a descriptive flyer
of Gloria Dei Lutheran Church
Huntingdon Valley, Pennsylvania

announcing the new
Gloria Dei Center for Creative
and Performing Arts

The Trend Towards a Popular Gospel

Rev. Stuart Briscoe, in a message given on John 1:9-12, said:

> When the church of Jesus Christ starts getting popular ... that's when you get worried ...
>
> When the crowds start flocking around the church of Jesus Christ, that is the moment of most imminent danger ... For it may well be that when it becomes popular and crowds come flocking, it is because they are being entertained by what they want to hear and they are rejoicing and getting what they want to get.

It could well be that the church ... the evangelical church ... has already reached this stage. Time alone will tell.

The liberal church has long since built its house upon the sand and it is very easy to identify. From basic theology to belly dancing lessons; from a recognition of sin to study in astrology; from a new life in Christ to a better life on earth.

What Is Our Direction?

It is easy to pinpoint the faults of the liberal church. And Bible scholars know that this ecumenical movement will someday result in a unified church headed by a False Prophet who will direct all allegiance to the world leader called Antichrist. But as the liberals go wild, are there also dangerous trends with orthodoxy which many evangelical Bible-believing churches are not fully aware of?

Dealer warning published in October, 1976 *BOOKSTORE JOURNAL.*

Rips Carter in sermon

Baptist pastor endorses Ford

By Aldo Beckman

Chicago Tribune Press Service

DALLAS—The flamboyant and controversial pastor of the largest Baptist congregation in America, Dr. W.A. Criswell, endorsed President Ford's election efforts Sunday.

There was a chorus of "Amens" as he said, "There are other public media through which we can discuss moral issues other than in the pages of a salacious pornographic magazine."

It was Democratic candidate Carter's Playboy interview that apparently aborted an expected endorsement of him from Criswell. There were reports that the ... several ... Playboy ... were

POLITICIANS ARE DISCOVERING IT'S O.K. TO TALK RELIGION

Once again, religion is an issue in a White House race. Contenders are discussing their beliefs freely. Big question: How will voters react?

For the first time since the Kennedy-Nixon race 16 years ago, religion is playing an important role in a presidential campaign.

Suddenly, candidates in both parties are talking openly about their religious beliefs, a subject that most politicians traditionally take great pains to avoid in national elections.

discussion with his sister, Ruth Carter Stapleton, an evangelist and "inner healer." Later, he did missionary work in the North. As Carter described his religious experience:

"I recognized for the first time that I had lacked something very precious—a complete commitment to Christ, a presence of the Holy Spirit in my life in a more profound and personal way. And since then, I've had an inner peace and inner conviction and assurance that have transformed my life for the better."

The former Governor of Georgia has denied suggestions that his personal faith might cloud his judgment in office or that he is using religion to further his ...

Churches' unification predicted

Leaders forecast end of 'lovers' quarrel'

Southern Baptists and Catholics Find Ties

By KENNETH A. BRIGGS

Every third Thursday, the Rev. C. Brownlow Hastings and six other Southern Baptist ministers drive a few miles from downtown Atlanta to a secluded Trappist monastery. There, with three Roman Catholic monks, they spend the day reading the New Testament in Greek.

Many Explore Ideas and Work Together, Though Some Distrust Remains

vation as an initial conversion or "born again" experience in which the person feels a commitment to Christ. "In our evangelical tradition," Dr. Broach explains, "it simply signifies your personal decision to be a Christian."

While some say the moment was a dramatic, even supernatural, experience, most, including Jimmy Carter, describe ...

We are witnessing the popularization of religion and serious efforts to unite all religions into one.

To Stimulate Discussion

The following remarks are meant only to stimulate thinking among responsible, Bible-believing Christians. They are not meant to condemn, but simply to observe the changing church and generate a positive forum of discussion that seeks to produce a more effective ministry.

Has Our Church Music Gone Down Hill?

<u>MUSIC</u> / Some 20 years ago there were some 30 gospel groups in fulltime activity. Today there are over 100. Some believe music trends are gravitating to a "rock and roll Christianity." They say that the sacredness and sanctity have disappeared. They believe that "Christian pop" music with its fluffy words lacks depth and encourages surface Christians who lack dedication and live on emotions instead of basic Bible tenets.

Are We Engaged In a Numbers Game?

LARGE CHURCH/TV MINISTRY Syndrome / Some believe there is a trend towards conglomerates for Christ. Big is considered good while small is considered bad. Small churches are expected to grow numerically or they are not "blessed by the Lord." Million-dollar-a-week ministries have cropped up. Some churches, caught in the "big church" syndrome have expanded so much, then they have gone into bankruptcy.

First Baptist Church of Hammond, Indiana (Jack Hyles, Pastor), is an example of a big church (over 4000 members) that *is* successful. Dr. Hyles personally counsels with anyone in his church who comes to him for spiritual help. Many try to imitate him. Some succeed, others fail. Should the evangelical church movement reassess its direction?

105

There is a definite trend in evangelization to imitate the world; in programming, in music and in presentation. Responsible Christian leaders will have to decide if such approaches are Scriptural.

**Do We Need
Stars To
Win People
to Christ?**

Viewers watch programs on television produced by what they believe are Christian leaders and become confused. Why does Christianity feature movie stars, people in high places who have broken the law and football players? Why has the Bible and Church format been replaced by a star-studded format? Is the Gospel such a simplistic thing of "... we got together and prayed and God helped us win the football game."

Have some Christian leaders been guilty of spawning a generation of lukewarm, surface Christians who lack the dedication of a C.T. Studd, a George Mueller or the martyrs who brought the Gospel to the Auca Indians?

**Are Some
Charismatics
Sacrificing
Faith For
Fellowship?**

The sudden, phenomenal growth of the charismatic movement . . . is it all God-directed and God-inspired? Or, again, does the desire for bigness overshadow the "separation" tenets of Scripture so that "love can abound." Are we willing to sacrifice what are the basic concepts and edicts of Bible separation so we can mingle with others under a bond of fellowship? Many Bible-believing charismatics are concerned about this unnatural growth that is diluting the message of God's Word and encouraging end-time ecumenicism that will one day welcome a False Prophet.

**Should Politics
and
Christianity
Mix?**

Why are those running for President suddenly putting on a cloak of Christianity? Why did the Pastor of the largest Baptist church in America openly endorse a political candidate during the 1976 elections? Is it not time for Christians to rethink their direction?

107

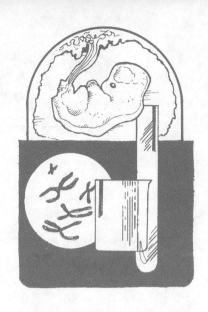

CHANGES IN SCIENCE CAPABILITIES

11:56

66 Have we the right to counteract irreversibly the evolution-
ary wisdom of millions of years, in order to satisfy the
ambition and the curiosity of a few scientists?

This world is given to us on loan. We come and we go,
and after a time we leave the earth and air and water to
others who come after us.

My generation . . . has been the first to engage, under the
leadership of the exact sciences, in a destructive colonial
warfare against nature.

The future will curse us for it.   99
                              Erwin Chargaff
                              Professor Emeritus
                              Columbia University
                              National Medal of Science winner

An Unusual Request

What action prompted the Cambridge, Massachusetts City Council to urge Harvard University to stop construction on a new one-half million dollar laboratory?

Prelude To Tribulation Judgments?

The reason: the laboratory was to be used for specialized genetic research. Scientists have learned to rearrange the basic genetic material of living things. By doing so, they have opened up an awesome field of science that could have dire consequences! The threat of a new mutant form of life which cannot be controlled and cannot be reversed is one that evokes fear worldwide. Could man himself be responsible for eventually creating the unusual locust of the Fifth Trumpet in the Tribulation Period that is able to sting like a scorpion but not kill? (See Revelation 9:3-12)

One Thousand Hitlers!

Genes are the basic unit of heredity. Through interaction with other genes they control the development of human characteristics. In other words, if science develops a way to control gene arrangements ... they could theoretically develop people on an assembly line basis that have the same identical characteristics. They could develop a nation of passive individuals or one of agressive individuals. Passive people would follow any ruler; aggressive people could fight fearlessly. They could develop a thousand people with the personality of a Hitler or of a confused drug addict. While responsible scientists would not stoop to such lows, Russian scientists have shown an extreme interest in this new ability to control gene development.

111

June 21, 1971 / 50 cents

Newsweek

PROBING THE BRAIN

Increased research is taking place on understanding the function of the brain and then controlling it. Through the power of mass media including the power of television subtle control is already taking place! Some 300 DNA projects are under way right now to control genes. And pharmaceutical companies are actively pursuing this research!

The Age of Building Human Robots

One University of Southern California biology professor said: "We believe that if you took an unfertilized egg of a human being, removed the nucleus and replaced it with a body cell from another person, you would get a twin to the person from whom the body cell was taken." This is called *cloning* ... the ability to reproduce an exact duplicate of a living thing. So far this has been done with toads and frogs. One day it will be tried with human beings!

The Dangers of DNA

This same scientist predicted that "... one day humans will exist almost like gods. They will have complete control of their personal destiny." He also believes that by 1984 we will be well on the way to developing drugs that will be able to control the body in any way we want to. Genes consist of double-coiled molecules which scientists term *DNA*. Successful control of DNA can determine skin coloring, muscle mass, hair, physical coordination, intelligence, and every other feature of the human body controlled by genes. A revolutionary scientific break-through on controlling human life is expected within the next 20 years.

The Sound That Controls

Scientists have also developed a strange, artificial high intensity sound that theoretically can wipe out brain cell memory, and thus wipe the mind clean and turn people into robots. The consequences of such technology ignorant in wrong hands is frightening. In tampering with nature, the future will definitely curse us for it!

113

11:57

❝ We now have convincing data that life was created from simple chemical substances in our atmosphere — hydrogen, methane, ammonia, carbon dioxide and water ... so any planet formed before Earth that also had these basic building blocks of life in its atmosphere is likely to be populated by intelligent beings more advanced than us.

We believe some planets are billions of years older than Earth — so their civilizations will be billions of years ahead of ours. It's a mind boggling thought, but I'm sure there are space civilizations so advanced that ours will seem Stone Age by comparison.

When we make contact — possibly within the next 15 years — it'll be the biggest breakthrough in the history of mankind. These advanced civilizations could help us conquer problems like disease, pollution, food and energy shortages, and natural disasters. ❞

> Dr. John Billingham
> Chief, Bio-Technology Division
> NASA's Ames Research Center
>
> Dr. Ichtiaque Rasool
> Chief Scientist
> NASA Office of Space Science

Seeking the Origin of Life

Man seeks to discover the origin of life. It is an eternal quest. Those that accept the Bible as the Word of God accept the Genesis account of the creation of the universe.

With the problems of ecology and a crowded Earth, many are seeking wider vistas to explore and to populate.

Twice in history a series of great voyages, compressed within a few decades, have vastly extended the horizons of knowledge. The first voyage began in 1492 with Columbus. The second, many believe, began when Viking 1 landed on the surface of Mars in July, 1976.

An Apathetic Public

For eleven months Viking 1 had whirled through the corridors of space bent on a mission nearly a quarter billion miles away. With pinpoint precision space scientists were able to guide this 1270-pound craft to its destination by remote control from earth. Such a feat was perhaps more incredible and amazing than man's landing on the moon. Yet the public was apathetic.

The World's Most Amazing Photographs

Even more amazing was the fact that Viking 1 had a photographic system that could take both black and white and color photographs and beam them back to the United States!

Already space technologists are looking forward to regularly scheduled crew operated flights to the Moon and eventually to Mars. The Mars round trip flight would probably take 3 years to complete.

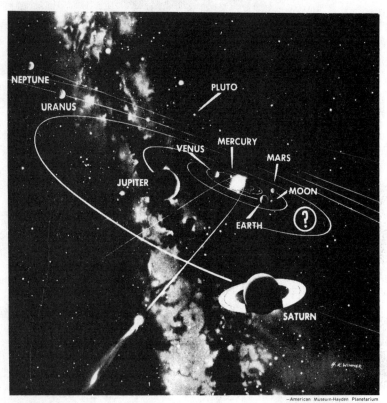

Scientists continue to try to fathom the dimensions of space. Recently, three Stanford University physicists appear to have found a "quark" — which they believe to be the tiny particle from which most of nature is built . . . the smallest component of matter. Scientists are still in disagreement on the "black hole" in space. They define a "black hole" as an area in space where gravitational pull is so intense that not even a ray of light can escape from its surface.

COUNTDOWN **11:57** TO RAPTURE

SPACE

UFO's Do Exist

Unidentified Flying Objects (UFO's) are increasingly becoming a subject of conversation among Evangelicals. Some believe they are messengers of God; others, messengers from Satan. There is a growing acceptance that UFO's are real . . . they do exist. But one should not believe they are messengers from God. For God has revealed only two types of creatures made to His image and likeness: angels and men.

In the End Times . . . Signs and Wonders

Matthew 24:24 tells us that . . . "false Christs and false prophets will arise and will show great signs and wonders, so as to mislead, if possible, even the elect." As these signs, such as UFO's become more convincing, Christians should be on guard realizing that nothing . . . neither death, nor life, nor angels, nor principalities, nor things present, nor things to come . . . nor any other created being, shall be able to separate us from the love of God, which is in Christ Jesus our Lord." (Romans 8:38-39)

We Are Here!

Under contract with the National Science Foundation, since 1974, a group of scientists, sit at the world's largest radio telescope in Arecibo, Puerto Rico, reading messages from stars, quasars and pulsars and broadcasting advertisements for the human race. The message is beamed toward a cluster of 300,000 stars called Messier 13, near the edge of the Milky Way, 24,000 light years distant (a light year is about 6 trillion miles!). The message: WE ARE HERE!

CHANGES
IN
MINOR WORLD
POWERS

11:58

66 I found a big stone
to throw at a soldier.
I'm going to get a gun
When I get a little older. 99
Belfast youth, age 10

Ireland War Drains Britain

For over 7 years Northern Ireland has lived under the shadow of gunmen. Their streets have been the cockpits of bloody guerilla warfare. Their heroes have been the men who lie in ambush along the darkened alleyways.

British Rely on Common Market

England has been borrowing heavily to pay its trade bill ... as much as $25 billion — equivalent to about 15% of the country's entire annual output. The British pound has suffered. After World War 2 it was worth $4.80. In 1975 it dropped to $2 and in 1976 it hit an all-time low of $1.50. Coupled with this, the Italian lira has also suffered a devaluation; and France is plagued with both inflation and unemployment. West Germany appears to be the healthiest economy among the Common Market nations.

Common Market Power Growing Rapidly

With a Common Market alliance, however, this group is expected to forge ahead sharply in industrial output and by 1990, quite possibly, surpass that of the United States. It is already running neck and neck with the Soviet Union in industrial might and should surpass Russia within a couple years. Its nearest competitor is Japan. The Common Market nations are growing at a more rapid rate than their competitors! And their power is increasing. Is this an indication of the prophetic fulfillment of Daniel's 10 nation league which will stand where the Roman Empire once stood ... and which will back the rising Antichrist?

Euromart OKs One Passport

Rome — (UPI) — Leaders of the European Common Market nations yesterday agreed to issue a single red passport for citizens of all nine countries beginning in 1978.

But attempts to agree

bers of the European Parliament — now appointed by national parliaments — in a single election May 7, 1978.

But British Prime Minister Harold

tated to set 1978 as the target date for the elections.

The other members of the European Economic Community are France, West Germany, Italy, Bel-

Common Market Designed To End National Rivalries

By JOSEPH W. GRIGG

London — (UPI) — The Common Market, a supranational grouping of nine of Europe's most highly industrialized nations, is an economic su-

million — "the largest trading and monetary bloc the world has ever seen," said former Conservative Prime Minister Edward Heath who led Britain's entry.

The Common Market was

In 1957 they set up the European Economic Community and Euratom to pool nuclear resources for peaceful purposes.

The Treaty of Rome provided for

and other member countries were scheduled to be removed after a five-year transitional period, now in its third year.

The community also planned poli-

PRO-ABORTIONISTS ON MARCH IN ROME

More Than 50,000 Women Denounce Pope and Moro

ROME, April 3 (AP)—More than 50,000 women marched through downtown Rome today waving their clenched fists and shouting slogans against the Pope and Prime Minister Aldo Moro's Christian Democratas for their opposition to legalized abortion.

It was the biggest feminist rally ever in Italy. Women flocked to Rome from all over the country and marched for three hours through the churches and palaces of old Rome, disrupting traffic. Most were young women.

Estimates of the number of marchers ranged as high as 100,000.

BRITONS ENDORSE COMMON MARKET BY LARGE MARGIN

67% in Favor of Staying in Community After a Long and Bitter Debate

By ALVIN SHUSTER
Special to The New York Times

LONDON, Saturday June 7—
The British h
whelmingly to
Common Ma
political deba
here for year
role in Euro
The final
tional re
the first
showed t'
voted "y
margin c
four pa
iom—F
and N
memb
Econc
Th
prise
the
The
tri
th
d'

as results were announced.
About 63 per cent of the
united Kingdom's 40 million
to the polls,

COMMUNISTS WIN 4 CHAIRMANSHIPS IN ROME CHAMBER

Positions Would Not Block Expected Financial Aid From U.S. and Others

By ALVIN

The power structure of European countries is rapidly changing.

Nationalism Disappearing in Europe

Leaders of the Common Market agreed to issue a single red passport for citizens of all nine countries. The countries are: Belgium, Denmark, France, West Germany, Ireland, Italy, Luxembourg, Netherlands and the United Kingdom.

Communism Gaining in Italy

In 1976, for the first time in Italian history, the Communist Party won chairmanships of committees in Parliament. The victory reflected the growing strength of the Communist party in the mechanism of Government. In this same period over 50,000 women marched through downtown Rome waving their clenched fists and shouting slogans against the Pope for his opposition to legalized abortion.

Russia Gets a Bigger Bite of Europe

In August 1975, former President Ford signed the Helsinki agreement at the Conference on Security and Cooperation in Europe. The agreement contained 30,000 words worth of pledges, but the document had no real legal standing and was binding on none of the nations that signed it. It strengthened Russia by finally officially giving them Estonia, Latvia, Lithuania and E. Prussia.

Russian domination of Europe is a fact. Today 1.4 billion people — 35% of the world's population — and more than a quarter of the world's land area are governed by Communist regimes in 17 nations. It is easy to see how the power blocs are building up for the final Tribulation wars.

11:58

66 Every day you'd see large groups of Hutus being marched to their deaths. You'd think they would have tried to escape or overcome their captors, but they never did.

I saw them loaded into trucks like sticks — one on top of the other, suffocating — but I never saw one so much as complain. And I heard people saying that, at the camps, if they were being shot one by one down the line, each man would just stand there and wait his turn. **99**

An eyewitness to some of
the more than 100,000 people
killed in the tiny country
of Burundi in central Africa
in 1972

A Sleeping Giant Is Awakening

Africa is a continent in turmoil . . . seeking new priorities and forming new alliances. This reshaping of a once-sleeping area may well be the preparatory steps for the battle grounds of the 7-year Tribulation Period.

Military Governments Abound

Presently, Africa is very unstable. Today, 15 African states are under direct military rule. In addition, the governments of Egypt, Algeria, Zaire, Congo and Togo came to power as the result of military coups. Of the OAU (Organization of African Unity) countries which have civilian governments, 29 permit only one party to function!

The last remaining colonial enclaves are in danger of disappearing as South West Africa (Namibia), Rhodesia and the Union of South Africa are under pressure to relinquish white control.

Colonialism Disappearing

Over 350,000 black laborers toil in the gold mines of South Africa for about 35¢ an hour. Some drill in 90-degree heat, 4700 feet below the surface in cramped quarters where the ceiling is rarely more than 3 feet high.

Misuse of blacks by many colonists over the centuries has finally lit the fuse to independence. And in the race to control their own nations, world powers are rushing in to have a hand both in power and in influence. Africa is a pot, ready to boil over!

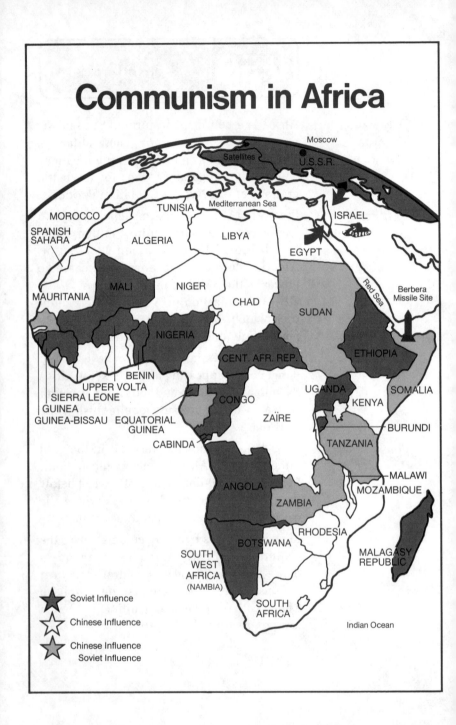

Communism in Africa

Moscow

Satellites

U.S.S.R.

Mediterranean Sea

MOROCCO

TUNISIA

ISRAEL

SPANISH SAHARA

ALGERIA

LIBYA

EGYPT

Red Sea

Berbera Missile Site

MAURITANIA

MALI

NIGER

CHAD

SUDAN

ETHIOPIA

NIGERIA

CENT. AFR. REP.

BENIN

UGANDA

SOMALIA

UPPER VOLTA

CONGO

KENYA

SIERRA LEONE

GUINEA

ZAÏRE

BURUNDI

GUINEA-BISSAU

EQUATORIAL GUINEA

TANZANIA

CABINDA

MALAWI

ANGOLA

MOZAMBIQUE

ZAMBIA

RHODESIA

BOTSWANA

MALAGASY REPUBLIC

SOUTH WEST AFRICA (NAMBIA)

SOUTH AFRICA

Indian Ocean

★ Soviet Influence

☆ Chinese Influence

⬠ Chinese Influence Soviet Influence

126

**Three
Power Blocs
In Africa**

Three power blocs are rushing into the vacuum created by changes in government in Africa: Russia, the United States and China.

**China
Influence
Increasing**

In 1975, China quietly completed the 1200-mile railroad that links Tanzania with landlocked Zambia. This $189 million rail link strengthens black independence in southern Africa and is a propaganda coup for China. China provided an interest-free loan, repayable in 30 years, starting in 1983. The Chinese faced some of the most difficult terrain but managed to lay 4 miles of track a day.

**U.S. Dollars
Arm Ethiopia
and Kenya**

Russia delivered over $200 million in arms to Angola in its two year war. While American arms sales to Kenya went from zero in 1975, to $7 million in 1976, and to $74 million in 1977 for F-5E jet fighters for that country.

Ethiopia continues to make large arms purchases from the United States . . . in one brief period . . . over $100 million!

**Russia
Keeps Eye on
Oil**

Russia has established a west coast stronghold in Guinea where Soviet naval units call regularly at Conakry's fine harbor, where they stock up on fuel and supplies for their continued patrols.

On the east coast of Africa, Russian planes and warships use bases in Somalia. From here they patrol the Indian ocean and the ever-important Strait of Hormuz, through which must pass all the vast supplies of oil from the Persian Gulf! It is easy to see why Russia has such a firm interest in controlling Africa . . . bases, mines and oil routes!

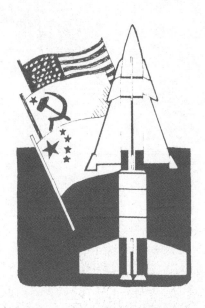

CHANGES
IN
MAJOR WORLD
POWERS

11:57

66 ... the U.S. economy of the late 1970's and the 1980's will be unlike anything the American people have seen in nearly four decades: an economy marked by slower growth, higher unemployment, and fewer fulfilled promises for nearly everyone. 99

Business Week
September 22, 1975

COUNTDOWN 11:57 TO RAPTURE — UNITED STATES

Television Debates An Ominous Sign

In the fall of 1976, two Presidential candidates, Gerald Ford and Jimmy Carter, faced the nation in a series of 3 debates. This trend of Presidential debates over live television is a trend that one day no doubt will help usher in Antichrist. Many people will judge a leader not necessarily on his ability to govern the country honestly and wisely, but rather on his ability to appear on television and without notes, be a formidable public speaker with a personality that is convincing. His smile, how he combs his hair, his ability to verbally rebuff his opponent . . . all will be major factors in electing him.

We are no longer living in an age when a Lincoln, born in a log cabin, can make it to the White House. It now takes money . . . plenty!

The Science of Becoming President

Political handbooks show how to create a crowd, how to pass out posters for the followers to wave, how to arrange television lighting to give a halo effect to the candidate, what to say, what not to say . . . how to appeal to the old, how to appeal to the young . . . how to appeal to the farmer . . . how to appeal to the businessman. Running for President is an exacting science. The President Ford Committee spent at least $12.5 million just to win the Republican nomination in 1976. And each candidate, Ford and Carter, spent $21.8 million to compete against each other. There is a tendency to promise anything just to capture the votes. But no President alone can achieve stability in the United States.

131

AMERICANS' GROWING RELIANCE ON GOVERNMENT

1 IN EVERY
5 JOBS
IS PROVIDED BY
GOVERNMENT

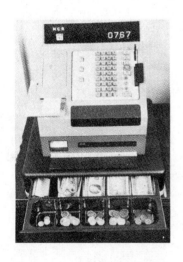

3 IN EVERY
10 DOLLARS OF
PEOPLE'S INCOME
COMES FROM
GOVERNMENT

**Unveiling
the Awesome
Power of
Government**

We are witnessing a "bureaucracy explosion." The awesome growth of the U.S. Government is, to those who are aware of prophetic Scripture, most frightening.

The Federal Government has become so huge that it is incomprehensible to the average American. Right now, over 5 million Americans (that's one in every 43 people) draw Federal paychecks! The Government employs some 3 million civilian workers in 11 Cabinet departments and 59 independent agencies, Congress and the federal-court system. There are another 2.1 million persons in the armed services.

The Government spends annually an amount equal to almost one quarter of the country's total output of goods and services.

**Land Owner
and
Controller
of the Purse**

The Government owns one third of the nation's land — 760 million acres. It also holds title to 405,000 buildings that cost $91 billion! It occupies 433 million square feet of office space. (This is equal to 96 Sears Towers, the 110-floor Chicago building which is the world's tallest).

Plus, the Federal Government provides the cash for one fourth of the total spending of State and local governments . . . over $60 billion. There are 4,504 different type of federal forms. The "official records" they generate each year would fill 11 Washington Monuments. The U.S. Government employs 211,000 secretaries and clerks just to handle the volume of paperwork!

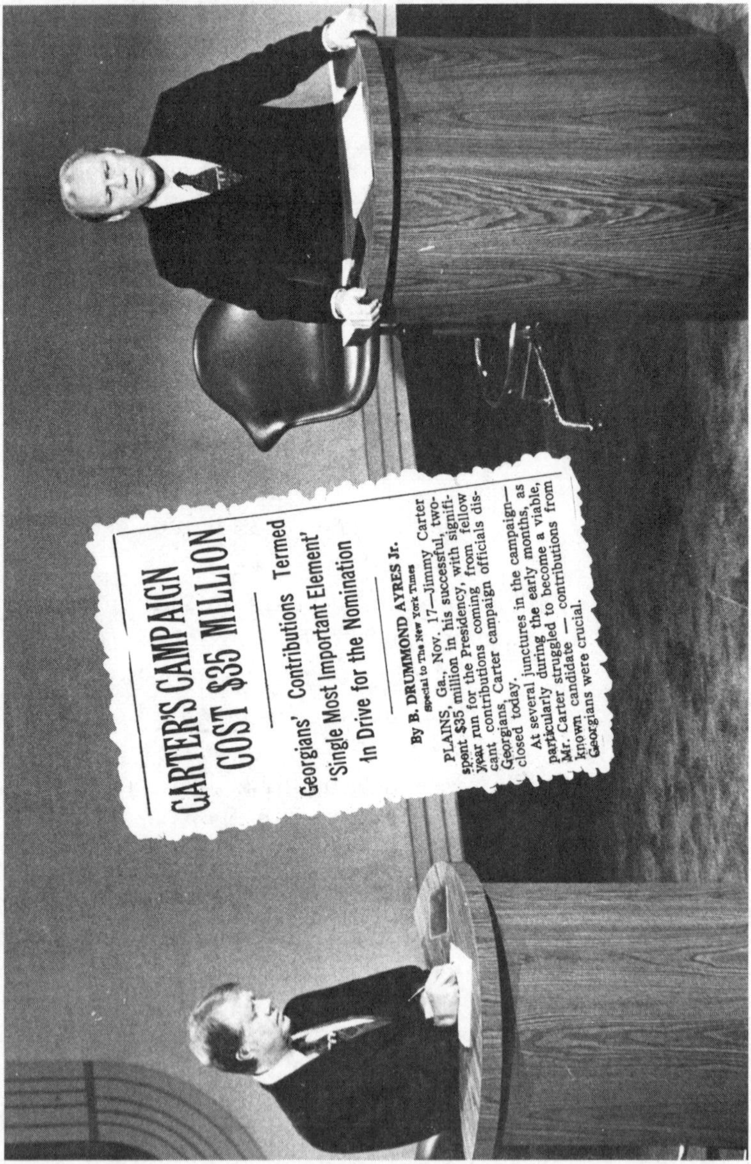
CARTER'S CAMPAIGN
COST $35 MILLION
Georgians' Contributions Termed
'Single Most Important Element'
In Drive for the Nomination
By B. DRUMMOND AYRES Jr.
Special to The New York Times
PLAINS, Ga., Nov. 17—Jimmy Carter spent $35 million in his successful, two-year run for the Presidency, with significant contributions coming from fellow Georgians, Carter campaign officials disclosed today.
At several junctures in the campaign—particularly during the early months, as Mr. Carter struggled to become a viable, known candidate — contributions from Georgians were crucial.

Jimmy Carter and Gerald Ford faced the nation in a series of debates. Each candidate spent $21.8 million to compete against each other.

COUNTDOWN 11:57 TO RAPTURE **UNITED STATES**

Government Power Increasing

The functions of the United States Government have multiplied and its power is worldwide.

Economy / The Government uses its vast power to spend, tax and control the money supply. It can steer the economy toward more jobs or fewer jobs, towards more inflation or less inflation. It regulates all interstate transportation, communications, electric and natural gas power, banking and the postal system.

Global Outreach / The Government's interest is worldwide. In 1976, for example, the President and his staff participated in more than 800 international conferences all over the world.

Science / The U.S. employs more than 232,000 scientists and engineers . . . actually one-fifth of the country's supply. This is four times the number that were on the federal payroll just 25 years ago.

Computers / A frightening statistic! The United States has the largest array of computer operators in the world . . . almost 12,000!

The Power of the President

The United States economy is bigger than all of Western Europe's and twice as big as the Soviet Union's. The control of the economy is basically in the hands of a few. The President of the United States is perhaps the most powerful man in the world. It is a power to be reckoned with . . . a power that eventually could go unrestrained in future years.

Panel Confirms Illegal Acts, Spying in America by CIA

Highlights of Rockefeller Panel Report

Bulletin Wire Services

Washington — The Central Intelligence Agency collected "a veritable mountain of material" — 42,500 files, reports, memoranda and cables — in an operation against American antiwar between

"no credible evidence" that the CIA was involved in the assassination of President John Kennedy. (See Page 4)

— The antiwar call Ch 200

— The CIA gave Americans kne

Bugging, Drugging Alleged

By NICHOLAS M. HORROCK
N. Y. Times News Service

Washington—The Central Intelligence Agency has conducted a vast network of unlawful or uncontrolled domestic operations that have resulted in files on nearly half a million Americans, mail openings, wiretapping, room bugging, burglaries, extensive "monitoring" of overseas telephone calls, secret drug testing and infiltration of American political groups, according to the Rockefeller Commission report.

The commission's report, delivered to President Ford on Friday and made public last night by his order, said the "great majority" of the CIA's domestic activities complied with the law. But, the report noted, there were incidents of poor judgment by officials, inadequate internal and external controls, meddling and pressures from Presidents Johnson and Nixon, and operations that "were plainly unlawful and constituted improper invasions upon the rights of Americans."

The report disclosed:

—In a seven-year-long "Operation Chaos" a secret group in the CIA conducted an espionage operation against dissident American political groups and created dossiers on 13,000

CIA Admits It Ignored Poison Ban

The Exotic Arsenal

In addition to the celebrated 11 gm. of deadly shellfish toxin and 8 mg. of lethal cobra venom, the CIA stockpiled eight substances that can kill people and 27 others that will temporarily incapacitate them. A sampling, drawn from an inventory that was made public last week at a hearing conducted by the Senate committee investigating the agency:

COLCHICINE. Paralyzes muscles, leading to asphyxiation.

STRYCHNINE. Commonly found in rat poison; kills by causing convulsions and failure of the central nervous system.

CYANIDE L-PILLS. Carried by agents in World War II; blocks the absorption of oxygen by the body's cells, resulting in an agonizing death by asphyxiation.

BZ. Blocks the transfer of impulses in the nervous system, resulting in paralysis.

CARBACHOL. Causes faintness, diarrhea and nausea.

SALMONELLA. Causes intestinal inflammation and dysentery.

HALOTHANE. An extremely potent anesthetic.

2-4 PYROLO. Causes amnesia.

M-246. Produces paralysis.

DESMETHOXY RESERPINE. Reduces the blood pressure; chronic use leads to severe mental depression.

CINCHONINE. An antimalarial drug; an overdose can result in cardiac arrest.

DEHYDROACETIC ACID. Impairs kidney function and causes vomiting and convulsions.

NEUROKININ. Produces severe pain.

Years from now we will learn of the intrigue and the hidden arsenal of deadly poisons that will eventually fuel the Tribulation Period.

The Power of the CIA

The Central Intelligence Agency (CIA) is just one of many government spy agencies. There are at least 4 government intelligence agencies that spend over $6 billion annually. They have even infiltrated through missionary organizations and American clergymen. One pastor was paid $11,414 annually as a spy. They have even opened up the President's mail. The CIA also tried to kill two foreign leaders and was involved in three fatal coups and kept deadly poisons in defiance of presidential orders! Some believe there is a trend to purge from the CIA, anti-communist personnel. In early 1976 former President Ford advocated centralizing his power (that of the President) over the CIA so that he would have more control over it. Such a step would further advance the power of the Presidency.

Monumental Defense Spending

Federal spending for defense will well exceed $110 billion shortly. And while the U.S. is spending increased billions for defense it is also doling out over $8 billion in major weapons to other countries. This makes the United States the top arms merchant in the world. The top 5 U.S. arms buyers last year were: Iran ($3.8 billion), Israel ($2.1 billion), Saudi Arabia ($588 million), Greece ($435 million), and West Germany ($220 million). However, these figures are constantly increasing!

Preparing for Armageddon

Meanwhile U.S. officials have ordered built six "doomsday escape" jets for the President and his aides and have hidden away $4 billion in new currency in a Virginia mountain.

6 PRESIDENTS AND RED INK

HARRY TRUMAN 8 Years
4 surpluses — 4 deficits
TOTAL DEFICIT: **$4.4 BILLION**

DWIGHT EISENHOWER 8 Years
3 surpluses — 5 deficits
TOTAL DEFICIT: **$15.8 BILLION**

JOHN KENNEDY 2 Years
2 deficits
TOTAL DEFICIT: **$11.9 BILLION**

LYNDON JOHNSON 6 Years
1 surplus — 5 deficits
TOTAL DEFICIT: **$42.0 BILLION**

RICHARD NIXON 5 Years
5 deficits
TOTAL DEFICIT: **$66.8 BILLION**

GERALD FORD 2 Years
2 deficits
TOTAL DEFICIT: **$105.0 BILLION**

Growing Reliance on Government Support

From the time they drink milk with their cookies in kindergarten ... until the years when they live out their retirement with the help of Social Security checks, most Americans get a helping hand from the Government. The Americans' reliance on government as an employer and benefactor has mushroomed to frightening proportions.

About 33 million people receive basic retirement or disability benefits from Social Security. The cost: almost $70 billion.

Almost 12 million Americans receive welfare. The cost: almost $30 billion.

About 20 million now receive Food Stamps. The cost: over $10 billion.

Fool-proof Identification System

Starting with illegal alien problems, Government officials are now working to develop an instant-identity plan ... a fool-proof identification card complete with the individual's picture that, when placed in a computer, could give a verification readout in a matter of seconds through a centralized computer station.

Regulatory Agencies Increase

Regulatory agencies in the United States cost the tax payer a total of $130 billion a year ... or an average of $2000 per family. The United States government employs over 63,000 people in regulatory functions covering some 20 different national agencies!

We are now in the era of more and more control; an era indicative of the last days.

The more man progresses, **the more he regresses!** In this modern, sophisticated age, it takes 5 people to change a light bulb in the city streets of Chicago at a cost of some $232 per light bulb change!

1   A city electrician climbs up and removes the outer globe.
2   Another unscrews and replaces the bulb.
3   A third person holds the scaffolding.
4   A fourth stands by with tools that might be needed.
5   The fifth is a city foreman who supervises the other four!

NATIONAL DEBT:
A SKYROCKETING SPIRAL TOWARD $1 TRILLION!

The Federal Government, officially, is permitted to owe only $400 billions. However, Congress regularly passes "temporary" increases in this limit.

The latest increase permits the limit to go to $700 billions. The tax-payers have to pay the swelling cost of this borrowing. In 1976, as an example, the Government spent 37.4 billion dollars in interest payments. By 1982, interest charges **alone** will hit $65 billion!

The U.S. wastes billions yearly on odds and ends:

$121,000 to find out why people say "ain't."
$37,000 for a potato-chip machine for the Moroccans
$68,000 to the Queen of England because she did not plant cotton on her plantation in Mississippi.
$2 MILLION to purchase a yacht for Marshal Tito of Yugoslavia!
$20,000 to investigate the German cockroach.
$5000 to the genius who wrote the 5-letter poem
                "light" (that's the whole poem!)
$13.9 million annually to maintain 300 military golf courses!
and on and on . . .

While you and I try to scrape up enough money to buy groceries and other common life-sustaining necessities!

11:57

66 The revolutionary people do not at all believe in so-called lasting peace or a generation of peace. So long as imperialism exists, revolution and war are inevitable.

Chou En-lai

Every Communist must grasp the truth, 'Political power grows out of the barrel of a gun.' Our principle is that the party commands the gun and the gun must never be allowed to command the party. 99

Chairman Mao

China Emerges As a World Power

There can be no question that Asia is under domination by Red China! China has been toughened over the years through suffering.

For years it was governed by two figures: Chairman Mao and Chou En-lai. Premier Chou En-lai died in January 1976 at age 78 of cancer. Chairman Mao died in September 1976 at 82 of Parkinson's disease and advanced arteriosclerosis.

Chairman Mao, since October 1, 1949, dominated the thought and actions of roughly one-quarter of the world's populace — the 900 million people of China. His plastic-covered Red Book, was carried religiously by nearly every Chinese citizen. Mao became the first leader in nearly 200 years to unify his vast country and make it a commanding power. To achieve this it is known that millions were killed.

An Agreement That Will Backfire!

When former President Nixon recognized Red China, it forced America's greatest ally in the East, Japan, to become an ally of China. It was a matter of political expediency for Japan. With the U.S. becoming friendly to China, Japan saw her ally (the U.S.) against China fading. Thus she chose to make friends with China. It is easy to see how the China-Japan bloc powers will have a major part in the Tribulation Period and particularly at the battle of Armageddon when the armies of the East . . . 200 million . . . cross the Euphrates River to challenge the powers of Antichrist (Revelation 16:12-16).

Chinese girls rifle training for future conflicts.

China Now a Superpower!

China's manpower and Japan's technical power will make a dynamic duo that in future years will spell trials for the West.

Chinese Army on Horses!

China is already a superpower. She has the world's largest military and paramilitary forces in the world. This includes an army of 2.5 million men with seven armored divisions, 119 infantry divisions and four cavalry divisions. Four cavalry divisions (men on horses) could conceivably be over 75,000 horsemen! What a picture of prophetic planning for the Tribulation Period!

Nuclear Capabilities Growing

By the 1980's China will have both strategic and tactical nuclear weapons including nuclear submarines. In addition to its regular army of 2.5 million it can easily recruit an additional five-million-strong militia force, which is already well trained and daily becoming better equipped!

The Chinese Strategy

China will continue to weaken Russia's political and military influence by promoting American interests where they serve the Chinese strategy. Once Soviet interest has been contained, China will try to weaken U.S. global power. She will try to create conditions whereby Russia and the United States get involved in conflict and inflict considerable damage on each other, leaving China as the sole superpower.

The Chinese are patient people and will devote years of planning to see their goals become a reality. They seek world domination.

145

U.S. Rules Bent to Sell 2 Computers to China

By LESLIE H. GELB
N.Y. Times News Service

Washington — President Ford, approving less than standard safeguards and making an exception to prevailing policy, has approved the sale to China of a computer system with military as well as industrial capability.

Administration officials said the sale of two Control Date Corp. Cyber 172 computers, which sell for about 12 million each, was approved as a gesture of support to the new Chinese leadership.

The officials said the United States did not intend to sell the computer system to the Soviet Union. Thus, the deal was an exception to the policy of selling to one of the Communist superpowers only what could also be sold to the other.

A National Security Council memorandum dated Oct. 12 and obtained by Aviation Week and Space Technology had recommended the lesser safeguards and the policy exception on the ground of overriding foreign-policy interests.

When the U.S. recognized Red China we forced our ally, Japan, to make peace agreements with Chairman Mao. We now also supply China with modern technology that one day could be turned against us. Pictured is former Prime Minister Kakuei Tanaka of Japan shaking hands with the late Chairman Mao Tsetung.

Japan a Growing Power

Japan, land of over 120 million people living in an area of only 143,818 square miles, is a power to be reckoned with. It was Japanese technology that created the "smart bomb" for the U.S. that always hit its target in the Vietnam War.

Rapid industrial development has brought severe environmental problems including air and water pollution. The Japanese would again like to expand their territory to alleviate the ever-growing problems of progress and population.

Living For Today

Most Japanese have a materialistic attitude towards life. Nudity on television was introduced in 1975 and gambling and abortion are an accepted way of life.

Dependent On Arab Oil

Japan's biggest vulnerability lies in its utter dependence on Arab oil. Japan relies on the Arab nations for 90% of its oil! Should oil be cut off, the nation would collapse!

Seeks To Increase Army

It is no wonder that Japan is seeking to increase its defense stature. It now has only a 238,000 man military structure, with about 500 combat aircraft and 450 ships (three-fourths of them, small). Their defense budget is only about $5 billion . . . less than 1% of their gross national product.

A Convenient Alliance

Their alliance with China gives them a military clout they would otherwise not have. And this strange alliance can someday soon cause tragic military confrontations in the future.

11:58

66 Détente is regarded in Moscow as essentially a transitory phase in relations between the Soviet Union and the non-Communist states pending the 'final triumph of Communism.'

> from an essay signed
> by eleven Western scholars

I wouldn't be surprised at the sudden and imminent fall of the West ... The West is on the verge of a collapse created by its own hands ... The situation in the world is not just dangerous. It is catastrophic! 99

> Alexander Solzhenitsyn
> Nobel Prize winner
> Russian author

COUNTDOWN
11:58
TO RAPTURE

RUSSIA

Communist World Grows

Throughout the world there are 121 Communist parties. Of this, only 65 are pro-Soviet. Another 30 are pro-Chinese (Maoist) and 26 are independent. The pro-Soviets (Marxists) are the most powerful.

Spy Network Increasing

Soviet agents (KGB) have managed to infiltrate U.S. government operations and are able to intercept and record phone conversations in the United States. Near the Russian-Finnish border the Soviet Union has been able to aim a mysterious microwave beam at the United States. American military experts believe that this strange beam keeps a round-the-clock watch on U.S. missile sites in the west and mid-west portions of America.

Bacteria Warfare Research Frightening

The Soviet Union does not live up to agreements. They violate the United Nations agreement on germ warfare by continuing secret research on biological weapons. It is believed that they have developed new virus strains (against which the world has no immunity) that are able to produce freaks or mutants. They also have spray guns with a capability of spreading enough germs around the country to destroy crops, kill off livestock and wipe out multiple thousands of people.

Dr. Vyacheslaw Stepanov, the Soviet embassy's chief medical diplomat, has shown an unusual interest in "genetic engineering" as discussed in a genetic symposium in the U.S. Many believe bacteria could be created that would be resistant to any known drug and could wipe out populations!

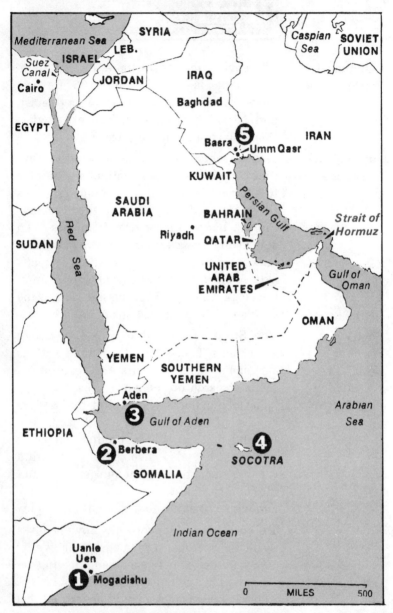

All Arab oil must pass through the Strait of Hormuz. This Strait is controlled by Iran. Watch for a power struggle!

Is the U.S. Now No. 2?

Is the United States now No. 2 in military supremacy? Many experts think so. The Pentagon believes, that in terms of the dollar, Russia may be outspending the U.S. by 50%.

Russia's Growth in Fighter Plane Power

A secret Pentagon intelligence study reveals that the Soviets, Chinese and their allies will have, by 1985, over 14,000 fighter planes, bombers and reconnaissance planes that will be within the range of U.S. naval ships and facilities. The U.S. navy, in contrast, will only have about 2500 tactical warplanes.

Soviets Outspend U.S. on Defense

While Soviet military budgets have been rising by 3-5% a year ever since the Cuban missile crisis of 1962 . . . the U.S. defense spending has dropped sharply (in terms of uninflated dollars) since the Vietnam war peak of 1968.

The Russians outspend the U.S. by over 40%, or $43.5 billion a year.

A Gloomy Prediction

Russian rockets can carry far heavier warheads than American missiles. Our missile gap is frightening. Malcolm R. Currie, Pentagon research director said in early 1976, "By 1977, the Soviets could theoretically, initiate a counterforce strike against U.S. missiles, absorb a U.S. counterforce response and then still have sufficient forces to attack Chinese and NATO nuclear capability, attack U.S. population and military targets and still have a remaining throw-weight larger than ours." Quite a gloomy prediction for the United States!

This Was 1972

President Nixon toasts China's Chou En-lai, 1972

The revolutionary people do not at all believe in so-called lasting peace or a generation of peace. So long as imperialism exists, revolution and war are inevitable.

Chou En-lai

From
PRIVATE NOTES,
1921

The capitalists of the entire world, and their governments, in the rush to conquer Soviet markets will close their eyes to the...realities, and will thus turn into blind deaf-mutes. They will open credits which will serve as a support for the Communist party — even in their own countries, and will provide us with needed materials and technology which will restore our military industries, essential for our future victorious attacks on our suppliers... they will be working for the preparation of their own suicides.

V. I. Lenin

DNESDAY, MAY 22, 1974

180-MILLION LOAN TO SOVIET UNION IS MADE BY U.S.

Biggest Credit Yet Extended by Export Bank to Russia Is for Fertilizer Project

By The Associated Press

WASHINGTON, May 21—The Export-Import Bank of the United States granted a loan of $180-million today to the Soviet Union to help finance construction of a huge fertilizer complex. The loan is the largest credit ever extended to the Soviet Union by the Eximbank.

The project, which was worked out by Armand Hammer, chairman of the Occidental Petroleum Corporation, include the import by the United States of ammonia and urea fertilizers from the Soviet Union in exchange for superphosphor

COUNTDOWN **11:58** TO RAPTURE — RUSSIA

Russian Aims Still the Same

Nothing has changed in Russian goals. They may couch their phrases in more polite language; rather than the Nikita Krushchev approach of "We're going to bury you."

Lenin spent most of his life in the West and knew it much better than Russia. He always believed that the Western capitalists would do anything to supply the Soviet economy... "They will fight each other to sell us goods cheaper. . . ."

Nothing has changed in Communist ideology. They have crushed country after country, upset the economy, caused chaos, then asked America "Help feed our hungry." And we did. We did provide relief during the administration of President Hoover through the American Relief Administration, through the Marshall Plan and we will do it in Vietnam.

Russian Power Deadly

As to dissenters — they placed tens of thousands on barges ... then sank them. They created an artificial famine in the Ukraine which killed 6 million persons in 1932 and 1933. At the height of Stalin's terror in 1937-38, more than 40,000 people were executed each month.

Clergy Infiltrated

Dr. Carl McIntire has fearlessly exposed the fact that Russian secret police have infiltrated the Russian clergy. Yet many American church groups welcome them with open arms. One day in the not-too-distant future the power of Russian communism will be found within America.

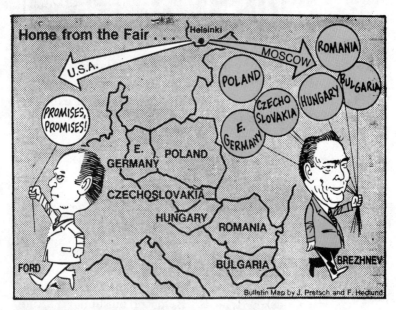

RUSSIAN MILITARY POWER
A THREAT TO PEACE IN EUROPE

MANPOWER		**TANKS**	
NATO	635,000	NATO	7,000
WARSAW PACT	910,000	WARSAW PACT	19,000
DIVISIONS		**WARPLANES**	
NATO	29	NATO	2,085
WARSAW PACT	67	WARSAW PACT	4,200

Although Europeans expected the European Security Conference in Helsinki in August, 1975, to lead to dramatic changes in both East and West ... there is continuing evidence that police-state controls in Russia and its WARSAW PACT bloc remain virtually unaltered. The Soviet arms build-up will eventually lead to an all-out war that will affect both Europe and the Middle East.

Preparing for Nuclear War

The Soviet Union has already had gigantic month-long drills of mock attacks on the United States. The Russians are already planning for a nuclear war and are constructing supersophisticated bomb-proof underground installations around Moscow. Many observers in the West are puzzled as to why the Russians would continue to arm in the era of détente. Soviet leader Leonid I. Brezhnev said in the winter of 1976, "It is all a monstrous lie from beginning to end. The Soviet Union has not the slightest intention of attacking anyone." Empty words, when one remembers Poland, Hungary and Czechoslovakia. In the last 10 years, while the United States spent only $804 million on civil defense, Russia has spent over $10 billion! The Kremlin's aim is to get into position to be able to fight a nuclear war and win!

American Capitalism Advancing Russian Communism

It is believed that almost 50 American companies are engaged in helping Russia complete a huge fertilizer complex near the Ural mountains. The fertilizer complex will cost over $4 billion. Chemical companies in the U.S. are aiding in the developing of chemical plants. Oil companies are negotiating to develop Russian oil. Other U.S. companies are seeking to help build an aluminum rolling mill in the eastern U.S.S.R. Lenin was right ... the capitalists will fight for the right to supply the communists because of financial greed! When will America wake up!

11:59

66 Hardly anything will determine the physical security of
American citizens in future decades more than the way
this country utilizes its economic, military and diplomatic
influence in shaping the worldwide development of
nuclear energy.

Like the rest of the world, the United States will have to
get used to living with new inescapable dangers. . . . By
the year 2000, the total plutonium produced as a byproduct of global nuclear power will be the equivalent of
1 million atomic bombs.   99

Report of the Research
and Policy Committee of the
Committee for Economic Development

**Laser
Death Ray
In the Making**

The development of a laser "death ray" as a military weapon is within the realm of reality. Both the United States and the Soviet Union are in a fierce race to be first with the killer beams. Laser beams can burn through bricks and melt holes in metal. Such a sophisticated weapon reminds one of the coming awesome Tribulation Period.

**Electronic
Warfare
Growing**

There is a growing use of electronic warfare. This is becoming a major military preoccupation of the defense establishments of the U.S. and Russia. Both countries spend almost $1 billion annually on electronic warfare and on further research.

**The
Gloomy
Future!**

By 1985, the Stockholm International Peace Research Institute forcasted that about 35 countries will be able to make atomic weapons. They believe that nuclear war will be inevitable! They have published a new publication called: "Armaments and Disarmament in the Nuclear Age." The publication paints a gloomy picture of far-reaching technical advances in nuclear, chemical, bacteriological and conventional weaponry. With about 35 countries having access to nuclear weapons it is easy to see how an unstable country, in an unguarded moment, could release nuclear weapons that could cause unprecedented disaster. Witness some of the erratic behaviour of Arab, Asian and African countries even now using conventional methods of warfare . . . and you can imagine the gloomy future that lies ahead!

157

STOCKHOLM, Friday, Oct. 8 (Reuters) —About 35 countries will be able to make atomic weapons within nine years and nuclear war will become inevitable, the Stockholm International Peace Research Institute forecast today.

The institute said also that scientists in both East and West were striving for a lead in nuclear technology that would make a pre-emptive atomic strike tempting to either the United States or the Soviet Union.

Parliament in 1966 to commemorate 150 years of unbroken peace in Sweden.

The publication painted a gloomy picture of far-reaching technical a in nuclear, chemical, bacteriolog conventional weaponry. It said th of nuclear capability to about tries by 1985 would be a by-p peaceful nuclear programs.

Stating that several "near countries felt themselves in gr because of their geopolitica stances, the institute predicted

sophistication "there will therefore arise many situations in which a successful pre-emptive strike will either be possible, or at least seem to be possible," it said.

Pentagon to Sell $6 Billion in Arms

Washington — (UPI) — The Penta gon has notified Congress it plans to sell nearly $6 billion worth of jet fighters, tanks

— West German F-4 fighter

Nerve Gas Seized in U.S., Austria Linked to Gangs

By WILLIAM BEECHER
Special to The Bulletin
Washington — Two chilling, unpublicized incidents, thousands of miles apart, raise the specter of gruesome new weapons in the hands

Ambassador Douglas Heck, chairman of a government-wide antiterrorism working group, said in an interview: "Libya is aiding, abetting and providing sanctuary to a number of terrorist movements. Libya has

A decision this summer to sell 250 Redeye missiles to Jordan is understood to have triggered a heated argument within the bureaucracy.

There is considerable concern about chemical and bacteriological agents.

Soviet missile drill above prepares for frightening developments in conventional weapons. While Pentagon researchers are currently working on a nerve gas that can cause agonizing death from only a drop or two on the skin!

**War is
Big Business**

Making and selling arms to foreign armies is so lucrative that more than 1000 U.S. companies are legally engaged in either producing or exporting weapons. The material is often sophisticated equipment such as laser range finders, night-viewing devices. The big corporations are well represented. Over 150 of Fortune magazine's list of the 500 biggest companies are engaged in arms sales. (32 of the largest 50 are included!)

Bulova Watch Company, Ford Motor Company, General Motors, DuPont, Gulf Oil, I.T. & T., U.S. Steel, IBM are among those engaged in making and selling weapons or weapon components.

**U.S. Policy:
Arm Both Sides**

The U.S. armed Iran with highly sophisticated weapons and fighter planes. When the Shah of Iran was dethroned, the Ayatollah Kohomeini took control. And on November 5, 1979, over 60 Americans were held hostage!

In 1980 the world spent over $300 billion on armaments. This is about equal to the entire national income of the poorer half of mankind. Over 400,000 scientists and engineers (roughly half of the world's total scientific and technical manpower) are now employed on improving existing weapons and developing new ones!

**A Sad
Commentary**

Since World War 2, literally hundreds of international meetings have been held in an attempt to control the nuclear arms race. Yet not a single weapon has been destroyed by international agreement!

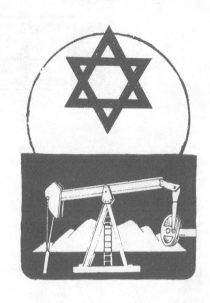

CHANGES IN MIDDLE EAST BALANCE OF POWER

11:58

66 If the U.S. were to totally abandon us . . . our very existence
would be in real danger. 99

Yitzhak Rabin
Prime Minister, Israel

Surrounded By Hostile Nations

Israel is a nation of almost 4 million people (of which about 800,000 are Arabs). The Israelis live in an area of 8,000 square miles surrounded by 19 Arab league nations of 4,991,000 square miles and 130.5 million people.

One Third of Budget For Defense

The annual Israeli $12 billion budget, by necessity, must include 38% of that budget for defense spending. They receive approximately $500 million annually from the United Jewish Appeal, $290 million in West German restitution to individuals and about $400 million in short-term commercial loans, and over $2 billion in U.S. loans.

Personal Tax Approaching 70%

Taxpayers carry a record burden. In 1975, 57% of their income went to taxes. In 1976 this has jumped to 65%. Average income is $3500 annually. (The people of Egypt have an average income of only $280 a year . . . less than the price of two tank cannon shells.)

Inflation is running at the rate of almost 25% a year. Foreign debt is over $8 billion and much of this debt is held by the United States. When during the 1976 election season, General Brown, U.S. Chief of Staff, remarked that Israel was a burden to the U.S., he unleashed a flurry of protest.

Lawlessness On The Increase

Suddenly Israelis also found themselves engulfed in waves of lawlessness. Police Minister Sholomo Hillel revealed that crimes of violence had increased 37% in 1976 over 1975. Tightening the belt was causing problems.

163

Must they wait for another Moses?

This Passover, Jews all over the world will celebrate the oldest of our festivals, by remembering how Moses led the children of Israel out of bondage...by remembering all the exoduses through four thousand years of history.

But remembering is not enough. Not enough for those Jews who today are denied the right to live as Jews—whose Passover must be observed in bondage. Not enough for those Jews for whom hunger, illness, loneliness and poverty are other forms of bondage.

Must they wait for another Moses? Who can be their hope?

We can, if we remember that we have survived for thousands of years because we have a tradition of helping one another. For those who are not yet free, we can keep the dream of freedom alive by keeping faith with them. For those who suffer in Israel, in New York, in other lands around the world—our immigrants and homeless, our children and our elderly, our deprived and dependent—we can be their hope and strength.

This Passover, we can be their "strong hand and outstretched arm." Let us give of ourselves to help Jews everywhere. Let us give generously, here and now.

Make a gift to the Regular Fund for our people in Israel, here at home, and around the world; make a special gift to the Israel Emergency Fund for our people in Israel.

Remembering is not enough.

United Jewish Appeal-Federation of Jewish Philanthropies Joint Campaign.
New York, N.Y.
Volunteer to be neighbors visiting neighbors on June 6.

A recent full page advertisement in the *New York Times* asks the question: "Must they wait for another Moses?" How soon will it be when Antichrist imitates the leadership of a Moses?

Israel Signs Common Market Agreement

In May, 1975 Israel and the European Common Market nations signed a trade accord to further strengthen their ties with the West. Prophetically one can see how such a tie-in with the Common Market and the United States could one day lead to an alliance with Antichrist (who will emerge from this 10-nation conglomerate).

Israel Major Arms Manufacturer

Israel itself has become a major exporter of arms. The arms industry in Israel employs tens of thousands of workers manufacturing everything from small ammunition to jet fighters. The locally made "Uzi" submachine gun is sold to more than 60 countries. Israel now exports arms to every continent and helps equip over 20 foreign armies!

Israel has also supplied arms and military assistance to the Christian faction in the Lebanon war of 1975-76.

Reverse Exodus Plagues Israel

Israel is suffering from a reverse Exodus. Since the birth of the Jewish state in 1948, 1.6 million Jews have settled in the country. Of this group, nearly 300,000 Israeli Jews have left Israel to live elsewhere. The reasons: rising prices, constant devaluation of the currency, heavy taxation, the always present fear of war, and a doubtful national future.

Even Russian Jews Leave

Only 8518 Russian Jews immigrated to Israel in 1975 compared to 16,816 in 1974 and 33,477 in 1973. Almost half of the Jews who leave Russia prefer to settle in the U.S. and nations other than Israel. The Government can do little to ease the problems that plague the economy. It is an uphill fight.

165

Try as they will, no leader or diplomat will be able to restore peace to the world. But the day may not be far off when a false peace will be manipulated by one who will later be revealed as Antichrist.

Meanwhile (see next page) Israel, surrounded by Arab nations, is like a pawn . . . whose fate lies in the hands of others. One can easily see why she would worship one who could bring peace between Arab and Jew after 4000 years of conflict.

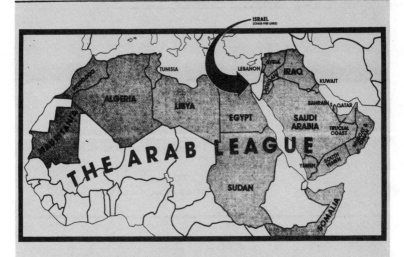

Nobody wants peace more than Israel.

Obviously, nobody needs peace more than Israel.

Israel is about as big as New Jersey.

It's surrounded by 20 Arab countries larger than the entire United States.

And while there are 120 million Arabs, there are only 3½ million people in Israel.

Of course, none of that has ever stopped the Arabs from trying to convince the world that they're just innocent victims of "Israeli aggression."

Or even from trying to blame Israel for the fact that there's still no peace in the Middle East.

But before you accept that kind of propaganda, look at the map.

If you were Israel, would you want war?

11:59

66 We do not want to destroy any people. It is precisely because we have been advocating coexistence that we have shed so much blood. **99**

Yasir Arafat
Palestine Liberation Organization

**U.S. Invests
$8 Billion
In Israel**

How far does U.S. commitment to Israel go? There is no formal American obligation to support or defend the Jewish state. Yet every President from Harry Truman to Jimmy Carter has firmly committed the U.S. to the survival of Israel. Since Israel's inception Congress has underwritten some 8 billion dollars worth of arms.

**Secret
Promises
of Support**

Secret accords between Henry Kissinger and the Israeli government promises ". . . to continue to maintain Israel's defensive strength through the supply of advanced types of equipment." Such weapons include ground-to-ground missiles and F-16 fighters. Also the agreement includes shipping of oil to Israel should Israel's supply be cut off. Some military studies show that Israel still holds a military superiority in the Middle East. Even though their military forces are outnumbered 2 to 1 by the Arabs, they have a "qualitative edge" in manpower.

**Playing Both
Sides of an
Explosive
Situation**

At the same time the United States is supplying arms to Israel, it is supplying over $1.2 billion in arms to Saudi Arabia. This includes, at the insistence of former Secretary of State Henry Kissinger, 650 Maverick air-to-ground missiles.

Thus the U.S. is being drawn into an even greater involvement in the explosive Middle East. The Russian move into Afghanistan in 1980 has further heightened the tension. The Egypt-Israeli Peace Agreement accomplished by President Jimmy Carter will not succeed. Look for a Mideast War to erupt in the 1980's.

Millions welcomed the then President Nixon on his June, 1974 tour of Egypt accompanied by President Anwar Sadat. Picture the tumultous welcome Antichrist will receive when he settles the Middle East conflict!

Mid-East Atrocities Shocking

The atrocities that have been revealed in the Lebanese war have been shocking as brother fights against brother. There have been mass killings of children and old people, with cruel mutilations of bodies. One housewife who witnessed the mutilation of an acquaintance said, "I don't care — they must all die." And over 50,000 did! Lebanon's population was only 3 million. From a comparative standpoint, it is as though the U.S. had suffered 4,300,000 deaths in a civil war! Such ferocity in fighting among Arabs who are brothers is a dark picture of what could occur if Arab is pitted against Jew in future soon coming wars.

Israeli Arabs Restless

Arabs within Israel are becoming increasingly more restless. For the first time in Israel's 28 years of existence, the Jewish state's large Arab population rose in violent protest in April, 1976 against a Government plan to take 6000 acres of land for development of a Jewish population near Galilee. In October, 1976 Arab youths took to the streets on Yom Kippur in a protest sparked by religious strife in the Biblical Arab town of Hebron.

American Jews . . . The Dilemma

Israel would like to see more American Jews live in Israel. There are about 6 million Jews in the U.S. (twice as many as reside in Israel).

In the U.S. Jewish people are suddenly tending to marry outside their faith at a high rate (almost 1/3rd of all Jewish marriages are now mixed). And 53.1% of Jewish households are not affiliated with any synagogue. These facts trouble Israel who needs all the support she can get.

171

11:59

(Referring to Israel)

" We have always been in conflict with each other since time began. And we will always be in conflict with each other till the end of the world. "

Anwar Sadat, President
Egypt
(In a televised interview
 with Barbara Walters on
ABC News, October 4, 1976)

COUNTDOWN **11:59** TO RAPTURE — **ARAB NATIONS**

For Egypt, An Uneasy Peace

Peace has not brought prosperity to Egypt. In 1976 alone, the Government had to import over $1 billion worth of food for its 38 million population. Because of housing shortages some couples wait up to 2 years to get married. Unrest could move Egypt into another mid-east war.

Saudi Arabia Growing in Power

Saudi Arabia is a growing power and a potential threat to peace in the Middle East. Saudi Arabia is considered by many to be the key country in the new Arab world. It hauls in about $30 billion annually in oil revenues and spends only half of it. In fact, it was Saudi Arabia that was able to accomplish something no other country could do; to get the presidents of Egypt, Syria and Lebanon and the head of the Palestine Liberation Organization to gather in the same city at the same time to achieve a peace in Lebanon.

U.S. Military Aid Substantial

The Saudi Arabia power comes from oil. It is the world's largest oil exporter and has the world's largest proven oil reserves (well over 150 billion barrels). This puts it in a position to extend large amounts of cash aid to governments it favors. It has given such aid to both Syria and Egypt. Overpopulated Egypt is also deeply in debt to the Soviet Union. It is forced to rely on Saudi Arabia's help. In the last few years the United States has sold a total of $6 billion in arms to Saudi Arabia and is now releasing Sidewinder interceptor missiles to that country!

THE OUTCOME OF THE CARTER MID-EAST PEACE AGREEMENT WRITTEN 2700 YEARS AGO!

The newspapers these days are filled with the Peace Agreement that President Carter has accomplished between Egypt and Israel.

In Egypt, President Carter has been hailed as The Man of Peace!

So much news has hit us so fast in the past few months, that it may be difficult for most to analyze these events in light of Scripture. While Commentators will expend endless words attempting to analyze these peace agreements, they will fall short of the answer . . . because the answer is in the BIBLE!

God Warned Israel

2700 years ago, Isaiah warned Israel about placing her faith in Egypt for help. But Israel has not learned her lesson.

Isaiah says:

> "Woe to them that go down to Egypt for help; and stay on horses, and trust in chariots, because they are many; and in horsemen, because they are very strong; but they look not unto the Holy One of Israel, neither seek the Lord" (Isaiah 31:1).

The leaders of Israel believe that a peace agreement with Egypt will be an answer to their needs. President Carter has persistently sought such an Agreement but it will not be worth the paper it is printed on! It will be the most costly agreement ever made in recent years!

Let's look at Isaiah and analyze the peace agreement in light of what was written over 2700 years ago!

1. Woe to them that go down to Egypt for help . . .

The most important prophetic statements on Egypt are found in the 19th chapter of Isaiah. It covers Egypt's downfall, its trials and its ultimate triumph and its final recognition and worship of Jehovah God.

Looking back into past history, Egypt faced a civil war which was followed by subjugation under the cruel rulers of Assyria in 671 B.C. They endured this for 19 years. A prolonged drought then gave Egypt economic ruin. The first 16 verses of Isaiah 19 deal with past history. The last 9 verses are directed to the future history of Egypt.

Egypt suffers under the Assyrians, then the Babylonians, then the Persians, the Greeks, the Romans, the Moslems and finally, she will suffer under Antichrist.

When Anwar Sadat, President of Egypt, initiated a peace plan by flying to Jerusalem in late 1977, he was playing a part in the tremendous upheavals which precede the coming of Christ (Daniel 11:40-43).

Hezekiah sought Egypt's help and Egypt failed them. Now,

Israel is seeking Egypt's help. And despite President Carter's persistence and America's financial aid to come, of over $4 Billion . . . Egypt will fail Israel again. You don't have to look in any crystal ball to figure this outcome. Simply read Isaiah 31:1!

2. Woe to them that trust in chariots; and in horsemen!

Israel, Egypt and President Carter believe the peace treaty can be effective because of the money and arms that will implement it. This will not be true, however!

Both Israel and Egypt will receive some $4 Billion worth of new military and economic aid during the next four years. The United States will build two new airfields for Israel that will run about $1 Billion additional aid.

But one must remember while Egypt has 40 million Egyptians . . . she faces an antagonistic 100 million Arabs!

And while the United States pours Billions of Dollars into military and economic aid for Israel and Egypt, RUSSIA will be pouring arms and military aid into the dissident Arab nations of Syria, Iraq, Jordan, Saudi Arabia, Libya and Ethiopia. And when this occurs, you will see the greatest holocaust the Middle East has ever seen! For President Carter, in bringing Egypt and Israel together . . . has actually crystallized a tidal wave of anger among its Mid-east neighbors. Israel's mistake, therefore, is placing her hopes for security on Egypt and in military arms and soldiers! This is what Isaiah is saying!

3. Now the Egyptians are men, and not God . . . He that helpeth shall fall and he that is helped shall fall down . . . they all shall fail together! (Isaiah 31:3)

The Lord warned through Isaiah that Egypt would fail and not only would Egypt fail but also the country she was helping (Israel) would also fail! This was true in Isaiah's time and it will be true today!

There will come a time when travel between Israel and the Arab nations will be unhindered by barriers of any kind. No need for passports. No trade restrictions. One must remember that in Scriptures, Egypt was often looked upon as a place of escape.

Abraham went to Egypt to escape the famine.

The sons of Jacob went to Egypt to buy food.

Jeremiah went to Egypt at the time of the Captivity.

Joseph and Mary took Jesus to Egypt to escape Herod.

But Egypt will not always be a place of escape. There are indications in Scripture that Antichrist will come in during the Tribulation Period and possess the treasures of Egypt.

Right now, you and I are witnessing the stage being set for the final drama just preceding the Rapture. When the Rapture occurs, no one knows. But we do know that each day brings us closer to the time when Christ will redeem His own!

4. . . . They look not unto the Holy One of Israel, neither seek the Lord! (Isaiah 31:1)

This is Israel's big mistake. Her confidence is placed in Egypt and a world leader. Instead her confidence should be placed in the Lord! She is pinning her hopes for peace on Egypt (a reed . . . which if you lean on it, will break; 2 Kings 18:21, Isaiah 36:6).

Because Israel's confidence is misplaced . . . The Israel-Egypt Peace Agreement will FAIL! And you can depend on that! All this agreement will do is to hasten a new and greater war in the Middle East!

However, in the 1000 year Millennium (which follows the 7-year Tribulation Period), these things will occur:

1. Five cities in Egypt will begin to speak the Hebrew language (Isaiah 19:18).
2. There will be an altar and a monument to the Lord at Egypt's borders as a sign of loyalty to God (Isaiah 19:19).
3. Egypt and Iraq will be connected by a highway and they shall worship the Lord together (Isaiah 19:23).
4. And Israel will be their ally; the three (Israel, Egypt, Iraq) will be together, and Israel will be a blessing to them. And the Lord will say: *"Blessed be Egypt my people . . . "* (Isaiah 19:25).

What a thrill for us as believers to be witnesses to this coming glorious time!

HOW CLOSE IS THE RAPTURE?

**Truth
Outraged
by
Silence**

It was Henri Frederic Amiel, the Swiss author, who said, *Truth is violated by falsehood, but it is outraged by silence.*

For too long, many who know truth have been silent on how close we are to the Rapture of the Church. Others have made irresponsible wild guesses as to dates such an event will occur. No one knows the day nor hour yet we are not blind to the converging of events that point to crisis conditions.

**The Age of
Religious
Entertainment**

Over 10 years ago the late Dr. A. W. Tozer said: *A great company of evangelicals has already gone over into the area of religious entertainment so that many gospel churches are tramping on the doorstep of the theater.* Some of us are guilty of compromising the Word of God to attract crowds, build our little Temples on earth and promote our ego. This is truth outraged by silence!

We are on shaky ground. And in these last days we should be the leaders offering the full power of the Gospel to a world in desperate turmoil.

What does the world hold for us between now and the year 2000?

The World Has Changed

As President John A. Howard of Rockford College in Illinois recently pointed out . . . it may be difficult for this generation to conceive that just 10 years ago:

Gutter language was rare on public platforms and in plays and movies.

Co-educational dormitories (at colleges) were unthinkable.

Most people had little worry about being out on city streets late at night.

Marijuana and other drugs were not tolerated.

The garbage we have fed into the minds of the people through television, through salacious books, through hollow foods and tranquilizers is now reaping a bitter harvest of confused, jumpy adults.

Superstitions are said to cost America one half billion dollars a year, including about $275 million in business lost because people will not leave their houses on Friday the 13th. There are about 80,000 superstitions in America today and Americans spend at least $130 million on superstitious devices.

Exotic Diseases Threaten

Exotic diseases such as Lassa Fever and Bubonic Plague are creeping over to North America. Meanwhile scientists are now busily engaged in research into genetic engineering. Such experiments may produce a cure for cancer but they may also create organisms that man cannot control. George Wald, a Nobel Prize-winning biologist at the Massachusetts Institute of Technology, has called this genetic research: *... the most dangerous experiments in the history of science.* The University of Princeton report on Bio-hazardous Research stated that: *As the techniques become more developed and familiar, they may be perverted by fanatics or madmen to manufacture and disseminate a doomsday organism.*

Those of us familiar with Scriptures can easily see the handwriting on the wall as the way is prepared for the coming Antichrist.

A Dangerous Trend

It was Anwar Sadat's wife, Jihan Sadat, who remarked about Egypt's overpopulation by saying: *I tell my husband he should pass laws penalizing any couple that has more than two children, like refusing free education to any beyond the second child or sterilizing women after they have had two children. Right now I am organizing a campaign promoting population control. . . .*

The Paradox of Economy

Men's actions are sometimes baffling. While Government talks about saving money, the Boston Federal Reserve Bank spends $387,000 for "art" to decorate its lobby. The Philadelphia Federal Reserve Bank spends $335,000 for two pieces of art. While the Federal Home Loan Bank Board plans a $50 million headquarters complete with skating rink.

Nowadays, anyone can become President of the United States . . . if he has some $35 million! That's what it cost for Jimmy Carter to reach that plateau. And several Senators spent over $3 million in their elections. At the height of the Carter-Ford race, more than 1500 people were on the Carter payroll. The average salary was $180 a week.

The Perils of Progress

By 1991 the United States will have 170 million cars, trucks and buses, or 69 for every 100 people! That's 36 million more vehicles on streets and highways than today! This will bring one third again as much traffic! So if you want to cross the street, you better do it now!

The world looks to the United States for its daily bread. But we no longer have the grain reserves to meet an emergency even within our own country. Meanwhile prices continue to rise. Several years ago when I wrote that bread would be $1 a loaf, it seemed like a long shot. But now it is already a reality! Each year in the United States some 2 million acres of farmland (slightly less than the combined areas of Delaware and Rhode Island) are removed from the nation's 400 million acres of arable land and replaced with what planners call "urban build-up." In terms of spending, the federal government spends $1 billion per day! The national debt is growing at a rate of over $1 billion per week.

Planned Wars

Meanwhile the world population goes on, feverishly killing each other (or planning to). Just 30-odd years after the end of the most destructive war in human history the majority of nations in the world remain dedicated to the notion that military strength is the best available means of preserving national security and promoting national interests. World military expenditures amount to $280 billion *annually*.

Praying for Death

Huddled among pines atop a small hill in the ancient Japanese capital of Nara stands a temple housing a Buddhist shrine. This quiet haven is broken by swarms of people, as many as 2000 a week, who come to pray for a painless quick end to their old age. Head of the shrine, the Rev. Choetsu Yamanaka claims that all that is needed to assure a painless quick death in old age is for him to bless the worshipers' undergarments. The 2000 or so who come weekly, bring their traditional wrap-around undergarments in neatly pressed packages to be blessed. The blessing costs $6.66!

A Changing Profile

At the turn of the century 1 out of every 24 persons in the U.S. were 65 or older. Today that figure is 1 out of 8. And most are dependent on social security payments which grow daily in inadequacy. Perhaps this new Japanese custom will eventually filter over to America.

Seeking Immortality

The Committee for Elimination of Death believes "death is an imposition on the human race," They seek ways to replace worn-out joints in the human body, research genetic reprogramming, freezing people ... anything to achieve immortality.

But true immortality cannot be found either by scientists freezing you, or by your taking a drink from the fountain of youth. It is found only through Jesus Christ who said:

> ... whosoever drinketh of the water that I shall give him shall never thirst, but the water that I shall give him shall be in him a well of water springing up into everlasting life.
> (John 4:14)

Merging Of Human Brain With Computer Envisioned

Boston (AP) — The computer of the future should be implanted under the user's scalp and become part of the human brain, a Rockefeller University scientist said yesterday.

"Ideally, the computer of the future should be an electronic extension of the natural brain functioning in parallel with some of the existing brain structures and using the same program and data languages," Dr. Adam V. Reed said.

Reed, trained in engineering and psychology, gave a paper on the subject at a session on man-computer relations of the ftutre at the 142d annual meeting of the American Association for the Advancement of Science.

ASKED BY reporters at a news conference about possible adverse use of such a computer system, Reed said:

"It is essential that people be able to use them for their own purposes rather than be imposed on them by the political structure.

"If the political system changes, and massive abuses appear likely, that would be the time to disappear from the society."

Reed conceded that it is conceivable "that thoughts could be injected" into a person's mind with such a system.

Before an implantable thinking machine can be developed, Reed said, there must be new knowledge about the location and operation of the brain's neurons and "the code of memory."

Carter warns of 'catastrophe,' urges strict energy conservation

A   The Evening Bulletin —— Thursday, March 17, 1977

Court Strikes FCC Ban on Obscene Words

Washington — (AP) — A U.S. court of appeals has ruled that the Federal Communications Commission may not ban indecent language on radio and television, even at certain times of the day to protect children.

The ruling reversed an FCC cision o 197

a record by comedian George Carlin using seven words generally considered obscene.

The FCC said it ruled against the station because the record was broadcast the a' n childr

radio communications and its own previous decisions and orders which leave the question of programming content to the discretion of the licens', the court said l deci

nity's needs, interests said the decision, w Edward Tamm. "To v' 'tev

Daily the newspapers warn us that our world is changing and that the day of accounting is approaching at a rapid rate. But most people cannot discern the signs of the times.

184

With such a dreary outlook a rash of today's new inventions will supposedly make living easier and bring about more leisure time.

A Look into the Future

We may see a nuclear-powered artificial heart. It is already being tested in live animals.

Researchers at Rand Corporation envision a "subway system" someday capable of carrying passengers between New York City and Los Angeles in just 21 minutes. The fare, about $50.

Automobiles may be run by computer control systems that need no driver.

Chemical transfer of learning is already in the experimental stage. It is now possible to extract the memories from one animal and transfer them to another!

Mercy killing will yet become an accepted mode of death and be termed involuntary euthanasia.

Computers will make possible hand-held, portable telephones. You will be able to make a phone call while riding in a bus or walking down the street.

Three-dimensional TV and wall-size flat panel TV screens are in the planning stage.

The Ultimate in Baths

And for the ultimate in comfort, Sanyo Electric Company in Japan has already created a "People Washer" Egg. It's an ultrasonic bath. The machine showers and bathes the body, cleans the skin, massages the muscles and dries you. All you do is lift a finger to start the machine. It goes through several cycles (like a

Believers can look for greater persecution in the years ahead. Many Christians may become martyrs because of their testimony for Jesus Christ. See Revelation 20:4.

washing machine) automatically. First, a warm shower, then an ultrasonic wash with bubbly warm water; then small rubber balls float in the water and massage your skin and relax your muscles . . . then the rinse and drying cycle.

But none of this will bring real satisfaction, nor real peace.

Natural Tragedies

We will be plagued by natural disasters. A truly massive earthquake will one day strike California and many thousands will die. Weather patterns will change causing crop damage and famine. Wars will increase. Crime will run rampant. And the world will be reaping the harvest of turning its back on God.

When will Christ Come?

How close are we to the Rapture of the Church?

Will it be 1980, 1984 or the year 2000? Only the Lord knows.

We are in the crisis hour . . . an hour in far more critical condition ecologically, than in the days of Paul. We have polluted our atmosphere, poisoned our bodies with the trappings of sophisticated living. Wars have become more vicious and more capable of carrying out mass destruction. Certainly Paul did not have to be concerned about nuclear warfare, or germ warfare, or chemical warfare . . . or the ability to kill people through laser beams or through powerful noise emissions.

Of course the Last Days began with Paul, but today we are some 2000 years closer to the return of the Lord to catch up believers . . . the Rapture (1 Thessalonians 4:13-18).

Evidences that surround us show us that this old world is on the verge of a nervous breakdown . . . and no amount of Valium can resolve the problem.

Based on these observations, it is my considered opinion, that the time clock is now at

11:59

When is that Midnight hour . . . the hour of the Rapture? I do not know!

Nor is it my responsibility to know.

It is my responsibility to:

(A) Point the reader to Jesus Christ as the only answer to eternal life.

(B) Challenge believers to dispense with the fluffy, cotton candy Gospel that is so prevalent today . . . and get on with the business of Jesus Christ, and seeking to uplift Him through our devotion, our sacrificial dedication, and our desire to live a Spirit-filled, deeper life.

If you do not know Jesus Christ as your personal Saviour and Lord, may I suggest you prayerfully read the next page.

Truth is outraged by silence. In my own way, I have written **COUNTDOWN TO RAPTURE** to break this silence so that Truth, through Jesus Christ, might prevail!

My Personal Decision for CHRIST

"Lord Jesus, I know that I'm a sinner and that I cannot save myself by good works. I believe that you died for me and that you shed your blood for my sins on the cross. I believe that you rose again from the dead. And now I am receiving you as my personal Saviour, my Messiah and Lord, my only hope of salvation. I know that I'm a sinner and deserve God's wrath and judgment. I know that I cannot save myself. Lord, be merciful to me, a sinner, and save me according to the promise of Your Word. I want Christ to come into my heart now to be my Saviour, Lord and Master."

Signed ....

Date ....

"That if thou shalt confess with thy mouth the Lord Jesus, and shalt believe in thine heart that God hath raised Him from the dead, thou shalt be saved.

For whosoever shall call upon the name of the Lord shall be saved." — (Romans 10:9, 13)

If you have signed the above, having just taken Christ as your personal Saviour and Lord . . . I would like to rejoice with you in your new found faith.

Write to me . . . Salem Kirban, Kent Road, Huntingdon Valley, Penna. 19006 . . . and I'll send you a little booklet to help you start living your new life in Christ.